Bible Atlas

Bible Atlas

Edited by John Strange

AMERICAN BIBLE SOCIETY
NEW YORK

Bible Atlas

Translated by: Erroll F. Rhodes

© 1999, American Bible Society

Danish Original: Bibelatlas (3rd. ed.)
© 1998, John Strange and The Danish Bible Society

Maps
Maps 1, 2, 6, 24, 27-48, 50, 57-64
© 1963 and 1978, German Bible Society, Stuttgart
Maps 3-5, 7-23, 25-26, 49, 51-56, 65-77
© 1998, Danish Bible Society

Photos
© Richard Cleave, except the following:
Maurice Harvey, p. 9 m.r., p. 12 r., p. 15 m.r., p. 57 m.
Helle Poulsen, p. 52 b.l.
John Strange, p. 12 b.r., p. 15 t.r. and m.l., p. 25 m.b.,
p. 54 b., p. 57 b.

ISBN: 1-58516-001-6

Bible Atlas - Eng. 107300
ABS - 1999 - 5,000

Printed in Denmark

Foreword

The Bible is a collection of texts which were produced in a particular geographical, political and cultural setting over a period of more than a thousand years. This setting is not the one we live in today, and many of the biblical texts are therefore difficult for us to understand without some appreciation of their background. This *Bible Atlas* is designed to help in understanding this background when reading and working with the Bible.

The *Bible Atlas* consists of four parts, each with a distinct character and focus: physical geography, regional history, biblical events, and Jerusalem's history and topography.

First of all, it is important to be familiar with the geography of the homelands of the biblical texts. The geographical maps show the varying landscapes, climatic conditions and the principal travel routes in and around the land traditionally called Palestine.

The second part consists of historical maps showing the political and cultural dependence of Palestine on Mesopotamia and Egypt; and later its relationships with Persia, the Hellenistic world, and the Roman Empire. Palestine was no isolated island. Politically and culturally it was a part of the Middle East and the eastern Mediterranean world, integral to a history that extended over a period of 10,000 years from the first agricultural settlements to the birth of Jesus Christ. The last of the maps here shows the extent of the Jewish Diaspora at the birth of Christianity.

The maps in the third part are of biblical history, and illustrate particular biblical texts. Non-biblical texts are also occasionally mentioned. For example, in discussing map 39 *The Kingdoms of Israel and Judah* reference is made to the temple relief in Karnak, Egypt, with a list of cities captured when Shishak invaded Israel and Judah (cf. 1 Kings 14.25). But primary emphasis is on the biblical text. All identifiable places and regions mentioned in the Bible are represented in the maps; where it is necessary, possible alternatives are indicated and doubtful locations are shown with a question mark.

Some maps are related to specific passages in the Bible, such as the list of nations in Genesis 10 (map 25), or David's career (map 37), the ministry of Jesus in the Gospel according to John (map 59), or the life of the apostle Paul and his missionary journeys (maps 61-64). It should be noted that these maps do not represent modern scholarly theories or reconstructions (e.g., possible alternative routes or sequences in Paul's travels), but just the information as presented in the biblical text. Each map is identified with the specific biblical passages it illustrates.

Exceptions to the rule are certain maps which do not illustrate biblical texts, but are based either primarily or exclusively on non-biblical sources. Examples are map 49 *Palestine in the Hellenistic Period,* map 53 *The Decapolis,* or map 56 *Palestine in the Time of Jesus.* Strictly speaking, these belong in the second part of the Atlas with the historical maps, but they are included here for the reader's convenience.

Finally, in the fourth section there is a series of maps illustrating the history of the city of Jerusalem. These also include reconstructions of Solomon's temple and of Herod's temple.

There are two indexes to the Atlas. The first lists the biblical passages associated with the maps, so the reader can easily find whether and where relevant maps are found in the Atlas. The second is an index of all the places named in the maps. These do not include all the places mentioned in the Bible, but only those which have been identified and can be located on a map (cf. the discussion for map 44, *The Districts of Judah under King Josiah).*

Recognition and gratitude are due Bo Alkjaer of the Danish Bible Society for the tireless energy and creative ideas he devoted to the production of this revised edition. I must also thank Joachim Lange of the German Bible Society, who contributed significantly to the revision of the Danish edition and was also responsible for the parallel German edition. Last and not least I am grateful to Morten Aagaard, General Secretary of the Danish Bible Society, for his lively interest and encouragement in the development of this new revision.

February 1998
John Strange, Dr. Theol.
University of Copenhagen

The American Bible Society gratefully acknowledges the work of the Rev. Dr. Erroll F. Rhodes for his careful translation of the text.

The spelling of names of biblical persons and places conforms to the usage of the New Revised Standard Version. Differences of the King James Version and the Good News Bible/Today's English Version are noted in the Index.

Content

The arrow indicates the perspective of the satellite data

Area of the satellite data

Satellite view of Palestine from the north-east. The picture is not a photograph in the strict sense, but a composite derived from digital data retrieved by satellite.

To the right (west) is the Mediterranean Sea and the coastal zone.

Parallel to the coastal zone is the Central Range of mountains running from Lebanon to the Negeb.

Between Lebanon and snow-capped Mount Hermon (lower edge) is the source of the Jordan river which flows into the Sea of Galilee (Gennesaret) and on to the Dead Sea. South of the Dead Sea the Jordan Valley extends through the Arabah to Elath on the Gulf of Aqaba.

East of the Jordan Valley (lower edge) is Mount Hermon with the Golan Heights and Hauran to the south. Further south is the Transjordanian Plateau broken by the Yarmuk, Jabbok, Arnon and Zered rivers. To the far south are the red mountains of Edom.

See maps 1, 2 and 24.

Geographical Maps

The physical environment of the people who wrote the Bible was a critical factor in the shaping of their culture.

The land itself formed one of the basic influences for its inhabitants, deeply affecting the way they lived, the cities they built, and the relationships between their cities. The terrain largely determined their commercial routes, and consequently also the development of nations and of international relations.

Climatic conditions were also profoundly significant. Their influence may be observed not only in the material development of the people and their culture, but also pervasively in their religious thought. It is hardly by chance that the gods of weather phenomena and the myths about them are common to all the Near Eastern cultures.

The geography and climate of Palestine are naturally central to a *Bible Atlas*. But the geography and climate of the whole Middle East must also be considered, because Palestine was constantly actively engaged with its neighbors throughout its entire history. It is situated at the south-west end of the Fertile Crescent, an arc which extends from the Persian Gulf to the Mediterranean following the low foothills of the Syrian-Arabian desert, and is just to the north-east of where Asia and Africa meet. Palestine is bounded to the north by a barely passable massif, and by deserts to the east and south, making it strategically significant as the narrow corridor through which all traffic and cultural exchange was channeled between Mesopotamia and the Nile Valley.

This first part of the *Bible Atlas* contains maps of the geography and climate of Palestine and of the whole Middle East.

A view of the southernmost part of the Jordan Valley, looking from the northwest toward Jericho and the Dead Sea. In the background is Mount Nebo and the mountains of Moab.

The Judean Desert, looking southwest. The desert covers the eastern slope of the Judean mountains where there is practically no rainfall. In the foreground is a wadi, a valley where some water from the mountains accumulates in the winter.

The coastal plain with the ruins of Caesarea in the foreground. Carmel is in the background to the north. The northern part of the coastal plain is called the Plain of Sharon, which owes its rich and fruitful soil to silt from the Nile.

A view from Upper Galilee toward Lower Galilee and the Sea of Galilee. The Galilean highlands, a southern spur of the Lebanon, are broken by deep narrow valleys.

1 Palestine
Physical geography

Palestine may be divided into four zones from west to east.

The Coastal Zone is narrow in the north, widening into the Plain of Acco, and south of the Carmel Range it broadens into the Coastal Plain.

The Central Mountain Range continues the Lebanon and Galilean mountains into the central mountains south of the Valley of Jezreel (the Plain of Esdraelon) which are broken by broad open valleys, and further south in the more forbidding mountains of Judea by narrower valleys, finally melding into the steppes of the Negeb.

The Jordan Valley, a part of the Great Rift Valley which extends from Turkey to Central Africa, is dominated by the Upper Jordan River which rises in the foothills of Mount Hermon to flow through Lake Huleh to the Sea of Galilee, and continues as the Lower Jordan River to the Dead Sea. South of the Dead Sea it becomes the Arabah Valley, which extends to the Gulf of Aqaba.

The Transjordan Plateau is called Hauran in the north, the Central Highlands south of the Yarmuk River, and Southern Highlands south of the Dead Sea. To the east of the mountains lies the Syrian desert.

Finally, a striking characteristic of the land is the series of transverse valleys from the Central Mountain Range to the Mediterranean and to the Jordan River from both the Central Mountain Range and the Transjordan Plateau.

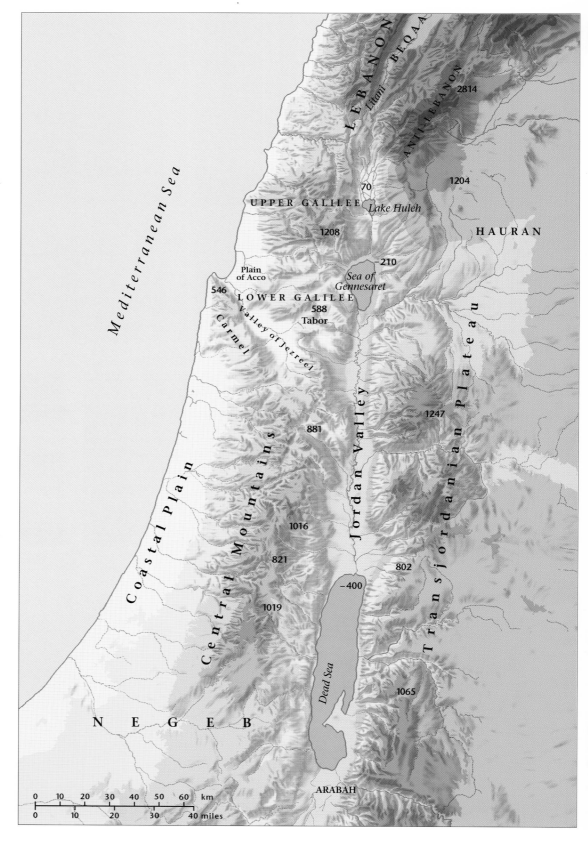

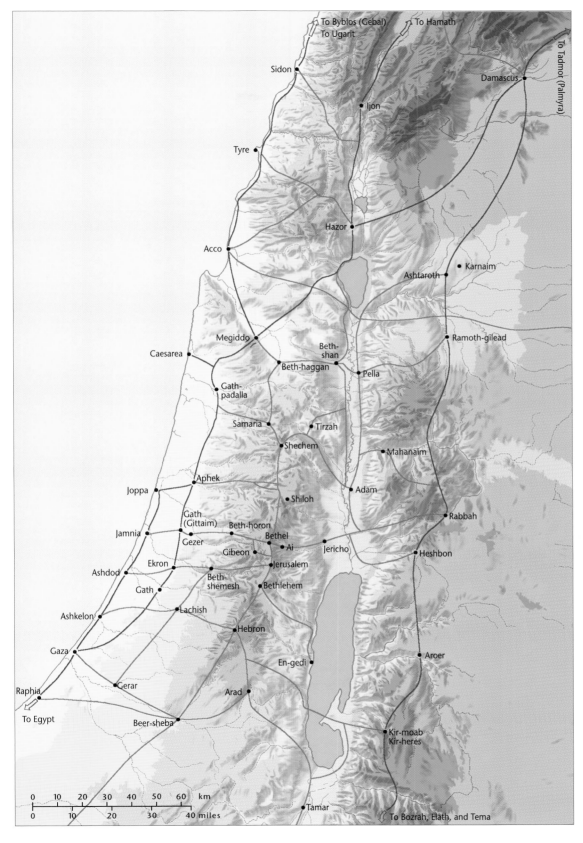

2 PALESTINE
Travel Routes

The highways in Palestine are dictated by the terrain and the climate. Besides the two major international routes – the coastal route (Via Maris, the Way of the Sea of Isaiah 9.1 KJV), and the King's Highway of Numbers 20.17; 21.22 (cf. map 6) – two further north-south routes should be mentioned: one along the crest of the Central Range, and one through the Jordan Valley. There were also several important cross routes, such as the road from the coast north of the Carmel Range, going through Megiddo and Beth-shan to Pella, or from Caesarea through Samaria and Shechem to the Jordan and on to Mahanaim, or from the coastal route through Bethel and Jericho to the Ammonite cities of Rabbah or Heshbon. This system of highways can be traced back to the beginning of the Bronze Age at the beginning of the third millennium B.C.

To Byblos (Gebal)
To Hamath
To Ugarit
To Tadmor (Palmyra)
Sidon
Damascus
Ijon
Tyre
Hazor
Acco
Karnaim
Ashtaroth
Megiddo
Caesarea
Beth-shan
Beth-haggan
Pella
Ramoth-gilead
Gath-padalla
Samaria
Tirzah
Shechem
Mahanaim
Aphek
Joppa
Shiloh
Adam
Gath (Gittaim)
Beth-horon
Rabbah
Jamnia
Bethel
Gezer
Ai
Jericho
Gibeon
Jerusalem
Heshbon
Ashdod
Ekron
Beth-shemesh
Bethlehem
Gath
Lachish
Ashkelon
Hebron
Gaza
En-gedi
Aroer
Gerar
Arad
Raphia
To Egypt
Beer-sheba
Kir-moab
Kir-heres

0 10 20 30 40 50 60 km
0 10 20 30 40 miles

Tamar
To Bozrah, Elath, and Tema

11

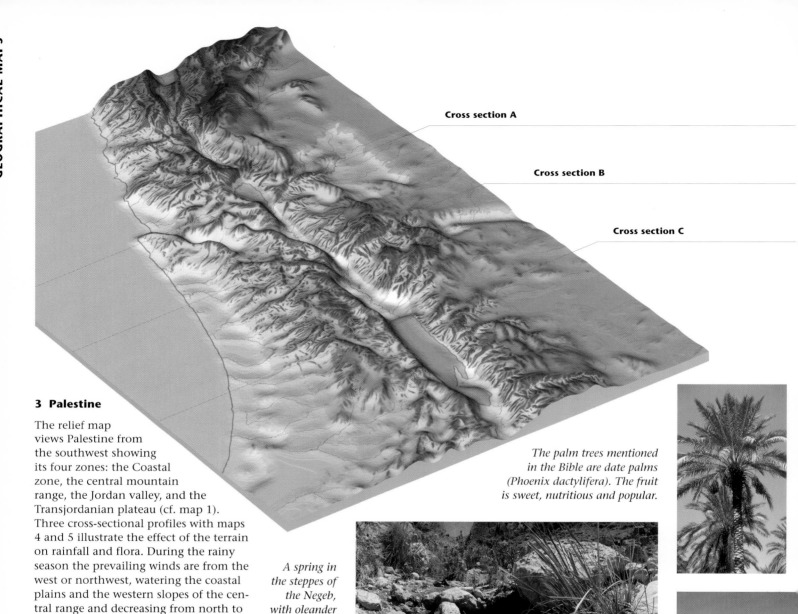

Cross section A

Cross section B

Cross section C

3 Palestine

The relief map views Palestine from the southwest showing its four zones: the Coastal zone, the central mountain range, the Jordan valley, and the Transjordanian plateau (cf. map 1). Three cross-sectional profiles with maps 4 and 5 illustrate the effect of the terrain on rainfall and flora. During the rainy season the prevailing winds are from the west or northwest, watering the coastal plains and the western slopes of the central range and decreasing from north to south.

The palm trees mentioned in the Bible are date palms (Phoenix dactylifera). The fruit is sweet, nutritious and popular.

A spring in the steppes of the Negeb, with oleander bushes and grass.

Occasionally solitary trees like this tamarisk are found in the desert west of the Dead Sea.

Oak trees in Galilee. Oak trees were frequently regarded as sacred, and play a significant role in the Bible, e.g., the oak near Shechem (Genesis 35.2-5), and the oaks at Mamre (Genesis 18.1).

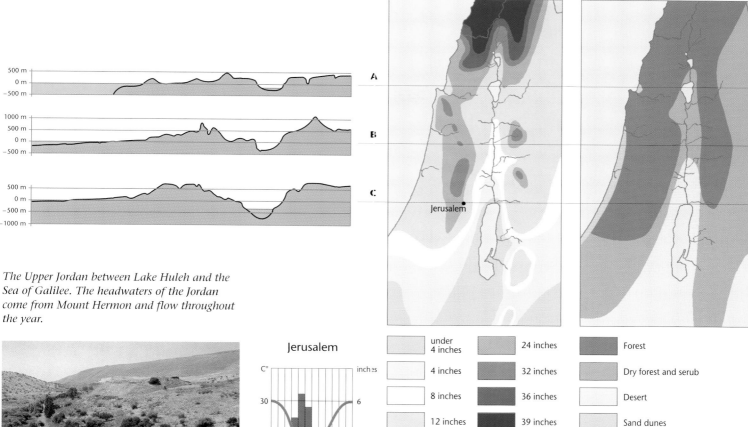

The Upper Jordan between Lake Huleh and the Sea of Galilee. The headwaters of the Jordan come from Mount Hermon and flow throughout the year.

Jerusalem

Temperature in C°	
Rain in inches	

The chart shows the relationship between temperature and rainfall in Jerusalem, with rain coinciding with the cold winter months and rare in the summer.

An olive grove in Lower Galilee in the spring. The cultivation of olives held an important place in the economy.

under 4 inches		24 inches	
4 inches		32 inches	
8 inches		36 inches	
12 inches		39 inches	

Forest	
Dry forest and serub	
Desert	
Sand dunes	

4 Rainfall

The map shows the mean annual rainfall in Palestine. The rain falls mainly in the mountains, especially in the northern part of the land. The 200-mm line is critical, because agriculture is impossible below it without irrigation.

The climate at the end of the Stone Age (Chalcolithic period, ca. 4500 B.C.) was more humid than today. Aridity increased in the Early Bronze Age, reaching its high point about 2000 B.C. Another period of drought occurred in the Late Bronze Age, between 1600 and 1000 B.C. Since then the climate has remained relatively constant.

5 Natural vegetation

This map taken with map 4 shows the relationship between rainfall and vegetation. Palestine is in a marginal zone between the desert and arable land. Even brief periods of drought over two to three years could result in crop failures and famine. This occurred frequently in biblical history, cf. Genesis 12.10; Ruth 1.1; 1 Kings 17–18.

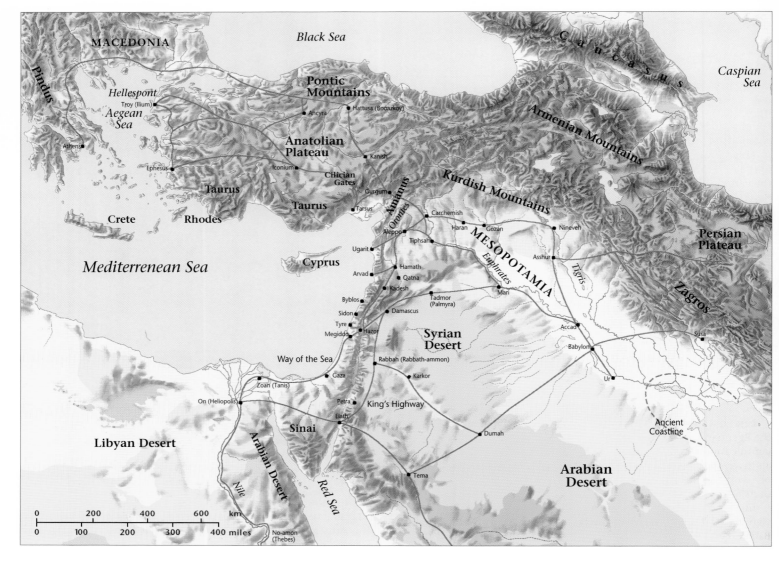

MACEDONIA

Black Sea

Caspian Sea

Pindus

Hellespont
Troy (Ilium)
Aegean Sea

Ancyra
Hattusa (Boğazköy)

Pontic Mountains

Anatolian Plateau

Athens

Kanish

Ephesus

Iconium

Taurus

Cilician Gates

Gurgum

Carchemish

Haran
Gozan

Nineveh

Persian Plateau

Taurus

Tarsus

Orontes

Amanus

Aleppo

Tiphsah

MESOPOTAMIA

Asshur

Crete

Rhodes

Cyprus

Ugarit

Euphrates

Tigris

Zagros

Mediterrenean Sea

Arvad

Hamath
Qatna
Kadesh

Mari

Accad

Susa

Byblos

Tadmor (Palmyra)

Sidon
Tyre
Megiddo
Hazor

Damascus

Babylon

Syrian Desert

Way of the Sea

Rabbah (Rabbath-ammon)

Ur

Ancient Coastline

Gaza

Karkor

Zoan (Tanis)

On (Heliopolis)

Petra
Elath

King's Highway

Sinai

Dumah

Libyan Desert

Tema

Arabian Desert

Nile

Arabian Desert

Red Sea

0   200   400   600   km
0   100   200   300   400 miles

No-amon (Thebes)

Kurdish Mountains

Armenian Mountains

Caucasus

6 The Middle East
Physical Geography

The major countries of the Middle East border on deserts to the west and south, and mountains to the north and east. A mountain range also extends from north to south paralleling the Mediterranean coast.

The foothills along the Syrian and Arabian deserts are forested mainly with oaks and pines. The great rivers of the Nile and the Tigris and Euphrates flow through the desert lands, making them irrigable. The whole area serves as a land bridge between the two continents of Africa and Asia.

International Routes

The routes in the Middle East conform to the terrain and climate of the area. Two major routes demand special mention. The coastal route (Via Maris or Way of the Sea, cf. Isaiah 9.1) connects Egypt with Assyria and Babylon. Beginning in Tanis it skirts the coast to Gaza, crosses the Carmel range at Megiddo and goes through the Plain of Jezreel to Hazor. Here it divides in two branches, one going north through the Beqaa valley between the Lebanon and the Antilebanon ranges along the Orontes valley

to Hamath, and then to Aleppo. From Aleppo it divides again, turning south to Tiphsah on the Euphrates and continuing beyond to Mari, Babylon and Ur, or going north to Carchemish and then eastward to Haran, Gozan (Guzanu) and Nineveh. From Hazor the alternative route goes to Mari by way of Damascus and Tadmor (Palmyra).

The second major route is the King's Highway (cf. Numbers 20.17; 21.22 and map 2), which goes south from Damascus to Elath and on to the oasis of Tema and to Southern Arabia.

Historical Maps

Most of the cities and towns mentioned in the Bible survive today as mounds of ruins called a tel in Hebrew or a tell in Arabic. Excavation of these mounds has yielded to archaeologists important information about the peoples and cultures of biblical times.

Just as the Bible was influenced by the physical geography of the countries which formed its environment, so also the biblical text shows the influence of the cultural environment in which it was written. This cultural environment had its deepest roots in the early agricultural communities that flourished in the Middle East after 10,000 B.C.

This culture assumed different forms through the centuries as various nations rose and fell. Accordingly it is important to be aware of the variety of cultural influences affecting Palestine in antiquity. In other words, what were the political and cultural relations obtaining between Palestine and its neighboring countries through the course of history? This second part of the *Bible Atlas* addresses this question with a review of the historical geography of the Middle East.

The following maps show that in the early Neolithic period Palestine took a leading role in the development of a material culture and probably also of religious culture as well. Later, in the Chalcolithic period (when copper implements came into use along with Stone Age tools), Mesopotamia took the lead. Great cultural advances were made, characterized by the building of cities and the invention of writing, bringing together all of Mesopotamia in a cultural unity.

Clay pottery are useful in dating the successive layers of materials found in a tell. Illustrated is a jar found at Tell el-Fukhar in Jordan, ca. 2000 B.C.

From the beginning of the third millennium B.C. Palestine became a bridge or gateway between the two great nations of Mesopotamia, with its great cities on the Euphrates and Tigris rivers, and Egypt, where Upper and Lower Egypt had become a unified state extending its political and cultural influence into southern Palestine.

Later in the second millennium B.C. Palestine became a part of the Egyptian Empire, and in the Late Bronze Age it was under Egyptian rule for about 500 years. At the end of the Bronze Age there was an invasion of the Sea People or Phoenicians, an Indo-European people. And with the destruction of the Hittite kingdom and migrations in Asia Minor there was possibly also a wave of Hittite immigrants.

In the first millennium B.C. Palestine was ruled by a series of foreign empires: first the Assyrian Empire, and successively by the Neo-Babylonian Empire and the Persian Empire, the Hellenistic kingdoms of Egypt and Syria, and finally in the time of Jesus it was a province of the Roman Empire.

All of these nations and cultures influenced Palestine and its inhabitants, leaving traces of their impact observable in the biblical text.

Caves in the desert at Qumran where some of the Dead Sea Scrolls were found. These include the earliest known manuscripts of biblical texts, mostly from the first century B.C.

Archaeological Periods		
	Palaeolithic Age	1400000 – 8/7000 B.C.
	Neolithic Age	8/7000 – 5000 B.C.
	Chalcolithic Age	5000 – 3500 B.C.
	Early Bronze Age	3500 – 2300 B.C.
	Intermediate Period	2300 – 2000 B.C.
	Middle Bronze Age	2000 – 1550 B.C.
	Late Bronze Age	1550 – 1200 B.C.
	Early Iron Age	1200 – 1000 B.C.
	Late Iron Age	1000 – 600 B.C.
	Persian Age	600 – 300 B.C.
	Hellenistic Age	300 – 60 B.C.
	Roman Age	60 B.C. – 325 A.D.
	Byzantine Age	325 – 638 A.D.

An inscription from Caesarea which mentions Tiberius and Pilate, the procurator who tried Jesus. The text reads: ...]S TIBERIEVM ... [PON]TIVS PILATVS ... [PRAEF]ECTVS IVDA[EAE] ...

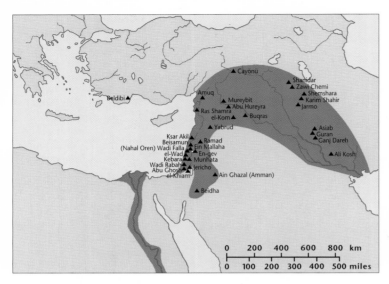

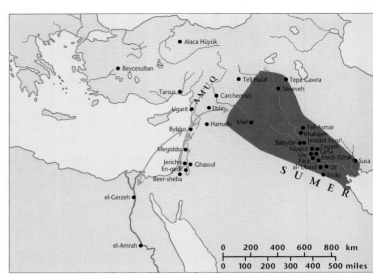

7 The Fertile Crescent and Early Agriculture

Native to the Fertile Crescent, comprising essentially the low foothills around the Syrian desert, were wild strains of barley, wheat, peas, lentils, pistachios, walnuts and beechnuts. Wild animals included sheep, goats, swine and cattle. The earliest signs of agriculture appeared in the transition from the Palaeolithic Age to the Neolithic Age, between 16,000 and 7,000 B.C. The map shows the major known settlements of this period, though admittedly much of the area has not been adequately explored.

9 The Earliest Cities and Literacy

The first half of the fourth millennium B.C. saw the development of the first cities in Sumer in southern Mesopotamia. Writing was invented and used in the temples and palaces. Originally the writing was pictographic, but it developed into a cuneiform that remained essentially syllabic, although it could also be adapted as an alphabetical script. The cultural influence of Sumer extended to Syria and Palestine, and beyond to Egypt. Only the most important of the cultural centers of the time are indicated on the map.

Archaeologists describe this as the Chalcolithic Age because Stone Age implements were being supplemented with tools made of copper.

8 Middle Eastern Flora and Fauna

The nine maps show the distribution of the most important flora and fauna whose domestication made possible the neolithic revolution. They made surpluses of resources available that were necessary to support the development of towns and cities (cf. map 9).

Wild barley (Hordeum spontaneum, vulgare)

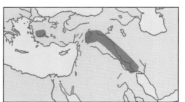

Einkorn wheat (Triticum boeoticum, monococcum)

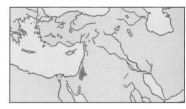

Emmer wheat (Triticum dicoccum)

Peas (Pisum humile, elatius)

Lentils (Lens orientalis, culinaris)

Sheep (Ovis ammon, laticaudata)

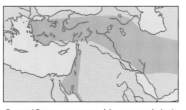

Goats (Capra aegagrus, hircus mambrica)

Swine (Sus scrofa)

Cattle (Bos primigenius)

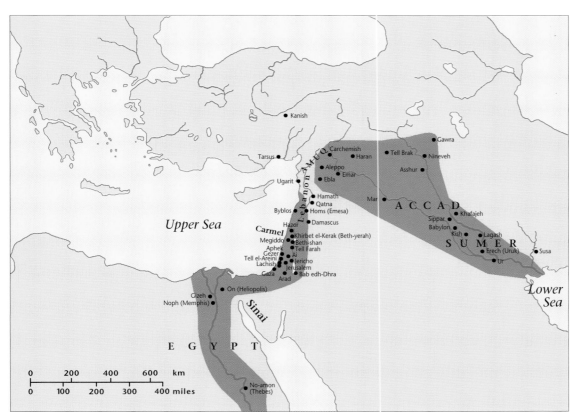

10 The Great Empires of the Third Millennium B.C. in Mesopotamia and Along the Nile

Shortly after 2400 B.C. Sargon of Akkad succeeded in bringing the whole of Mesopotamia under his control. One of his successors, Naram-sin (2291-2255 B.C.), conquered Ebla and advanced as far as the Mediterranean. His rule extended from the "Upper Sea" (the Mediterranean) to the "Lower Sea" (the Persian Gulf).

The "Two Lands" of (South and North) Egypt had been united as a single kingdom since about 3000 B.C., ruled by the kings of dynasties IV and V who built the pyramids. Their influence reached northward into Palestine and Syria.

Archaeologically this period marked the Early Bronze Age.

11 Hammurabi of Babylon. The Middle Kingdom in Egypt

The Early Bronze Age was followed by a First Intermediate Period, when the empires of the Fertile Crescent collapsed and their cities were devastated. Broad expanses turned to the nomadic life. Then under Hammurabi of Babylon (1772-1750 B.C.) Mesopotamia was again united and enjoyed a cultural renaissance.

In Egypt the kings of dynasties XI and XII expanded their influence northward as far as Byblos.

In the archaeology of Palestine this was part of the Middle Bronze Age.

12 The Egyptian Empire in the Near East

In a Second Intermediate Period a part of Egypt was ruled by foreigners, the Asiatic Hyksos (15th dynasty), who made Avaris in the eastern delta their capital. But about 1550 B.C. the first kings of 18th dynasty were able to expel the foreigners and reunify Egypt. The succeeding kings, especially Tutmose III (1457-1425 B.C.), conquered Palestine and Syria to make Egypt a great power, dominating the lands of the eastern Mediterranean and the Near East.

Archaeologically this marked the beginning of the Late Bronze Age.

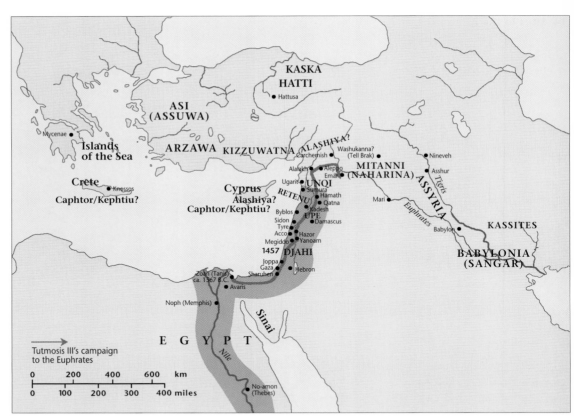

13 The International Balance of Power, ca. 1400 B.C.

About 1400 B.C. the Middle East was divided into a number of regions, each with an established monarchy. Relations between the regions were governed by treaties, inter-dynastic marriages, and exchanges of technicians (e.g. physicians and architects) and of material gifts. Interregional commerce flourished, and within each region commerce was generally a royal monopoly. Palestine was a province of the Egyptian empire, which was at the peak of its power under Amenophis III (1390-1352 B.C.).

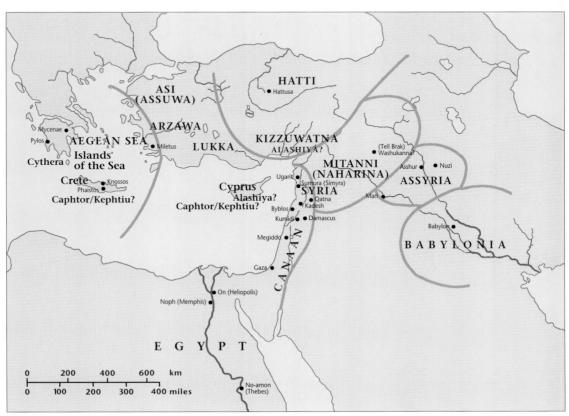

14 Sites in the Amarna Archives

During the reign of Amenophis IV (1352-1336 B.C.), also known as Akhenaton, the royal residence was moved from Thebes to Akhetaton, today known as Tell el-Amarna, where an archive comprising some 400 letters written in cuneiform on clay tablets has been discovered. Some were addressed to the Egyptian pharaoh by rulers of the other great powers of Babylon, Mitanni and Hittites, but they were mainly from vassal kings in Palestine and Syria. These letters reveal insights into the political relationships of the Late Bronze Age, especially during the twenty years covered by the archive – the Amarna period.

The map gives the names of places in their later biblical forms where possible. Not all the names in the correspondence are shown, however, as many have not yet been identified.

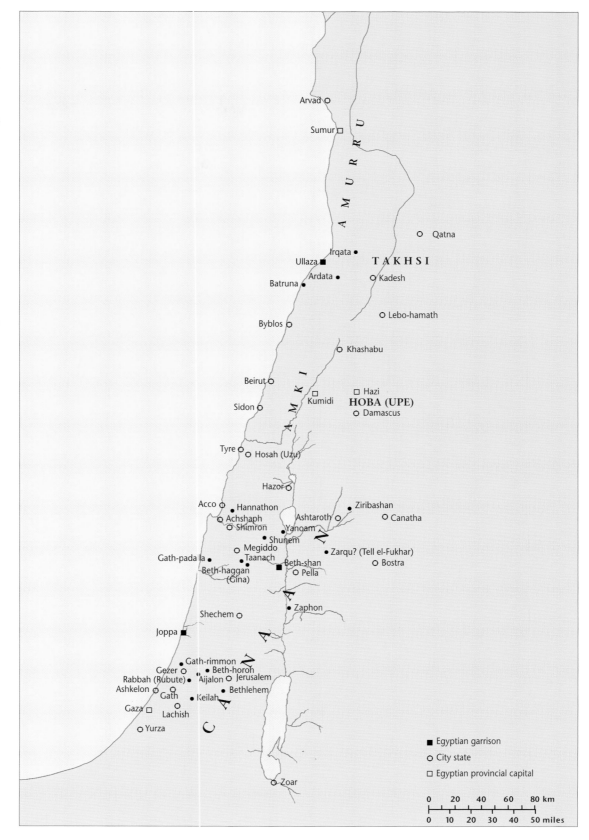

15 Rameses II and III. The End of the Bronze Age

After the Amarna period the kings of dynasties XIX and XX attempted to reassert their power in the Near East by a series of military campaigns and establishing garrisons in the region. At the same time the Hittite kings were expanding their rule to the west and south, resulting in a series of wars. Following the battle of Kadesh on the Orontes in 1259 B.C., a boundary line was established by treaty. But the crisis of a growing population with social and economic problems made the Near East vulnerable to foreign invaders, leading to a collapse of the Bronze Age states and the beginning of a new intermediate period.

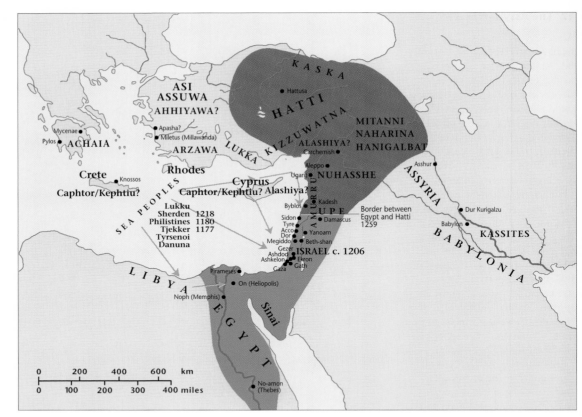

16 The Middle East ca. 1000 B.C.

About 1000 B.C. Egypt, Assyria, and Babylon were in weakened conditions, and the Hittite and Mitanni kingdoms had disappeared. This power vacuum spawned a range of small territorial states, some with Hittite princes and Aramaic peoples, some like Israel, Damascus, and Moab, and some city-states like the five cities of the Philistines. The dominant element were the Arameans, who were spread over a broad area from northeast Syria to the mouth of the Euphrates River.

In the archaeology of Palestine, about 1200 B.C. marked the beginning of the Iron Age.

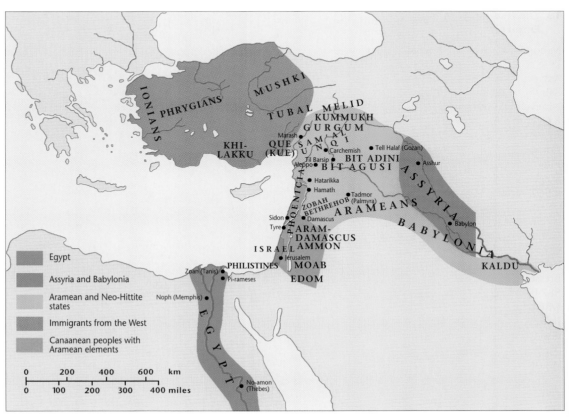

17 The Assyrian Empire

After several centuries of inaction, Assyria began about 900 B.C. to expand aggressively under Adad-nirari II, and over the course of 250 years it developed into the first great world power in history. The kings consolidated the empire by systematically relocating conquered peoples to destroy their national loyalties and emphasize their dependence on the Assyrian authority. The empire enjoyed its peak under Asshurbanipal (669-630 B.C.), and then rapidly disintegrated. Egypt achieved independence of Assyria in 664 B.C. under the Saite XXVI dynasty.

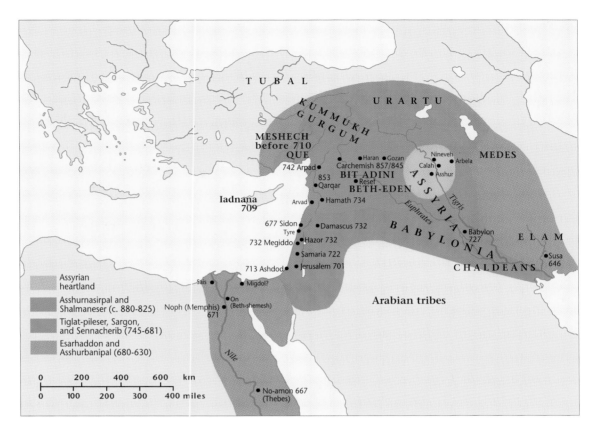

18 The Neo-Babylonian Empire

Nabopolassar was proclaimed king of Babylonia in 626 B.C. Assyria then faced a coalition of Babylonia, Media, and Elam. Nineveh was destroyed in 612 B.C. Egypt sought to support Assyria, sending an expeditionary force. Josiah, king of Judah, engaged this force at Megiddo in 609 B.C., but was killed. In the final battle at Carchemish in 605 B.C. Assyria and its allies were defeated, and Babylon became the ruling power of the Middle East. Nebuchadnezzar II (605-562 B.C.) suppressed rebellions in 598 and 587 B.C., including in Judah where he besieged and destroyed Jerusalem. In 568 B.C. Egypt also fell to his conquest.

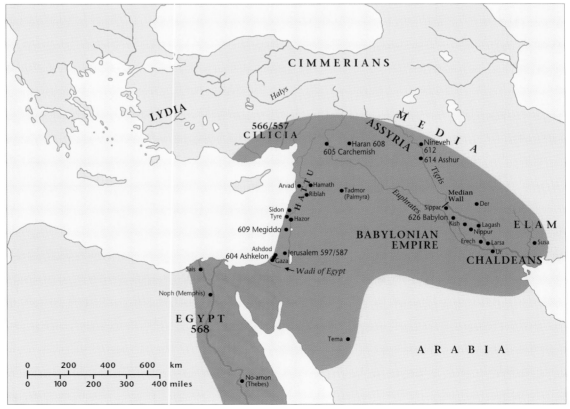

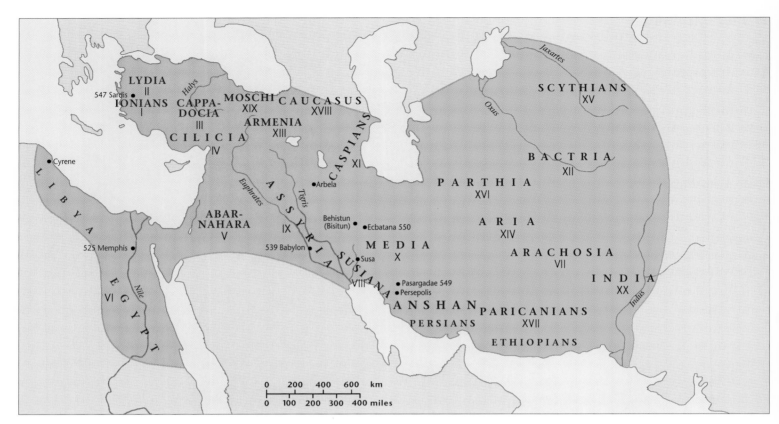

LYDIA
II
547 Sardis
IONIANS
I
CAPPA-
DOCIA
III
MOSCHI
XIX
CAUCASUS
XVIII
Halys
ARMENIA
XIII
CILICIA
IV
CASPIANS
XI
SCYTHIANS
XV
Oxus
Jaxartes
BACTRIA
XII
Cyrene
Euphrates
ASSYRIA
Tigris
Arbela
PARTHIA
XVI
LIBYA
ABAR-
NAHARA
V
IX
Behistun
(Bisitun)
Ecbatana 550
ARIA
XIV
525 Memphis
539 Babylon
SUSIANA
Susa
MEDIA
X
ARACHOSIA
VII
INDIA
XX
Nile
EGYPT
VI
VIII
Pasargadae 549
Persepolis
ANSHAN
PERSIANS
PARICANIANS
XVII
Indus
ETHIOPIANS

0 200 400 600 km
0 100 200 300 400 miles

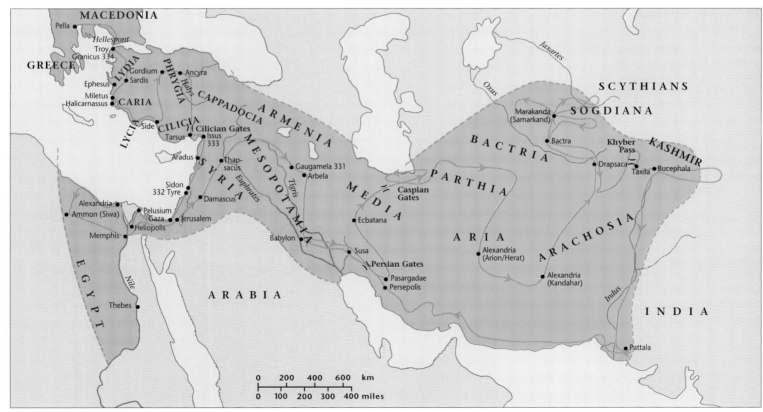

MACEDONIA
Pella
Hellespont
Troy
Granicus 334
GREECE
Ephesus
Miletus
Halicarnassus
LYDIA
Gordium
Sardis
CARIA
PHRYGIA
Halys
Ancyra
CAPPADOCIA
ARMENIA
LYCIA
Side
CILICIA
Tarsus
Cilician Gates
Issus
333
Aradus
SYRIA
Thap-
sacus
MESOPOTAMIA
Euphrates
Gaugamela 331
Arbela
Tigris
MEDIA
Caspian
Gates
PARTHIA
SCYTHIANS
Oxus
Jaxartes
Marakanda
(Samarkand)
SOGDIANA
BACTRIA
Bactra
Khyber
Pass
KASHMIR
Drapsaca
Taxila
Bucephala
Sidon
332 Tyre
Damascus
Alexandria
Ammon (Siwa)
Pelusium
Gaza
Jerusalem
Heliopolis
Memphis
Ecbatana
Babylon
Susa
Persian Gates
ARIA
Alexandria
(Arion/Herat)
ARACHOSIA
Alexandria
(Kandahar)
Indus
EGYPT
Nile
ARABIA
Pasargadae
Persepolis
INDIA
Thebes
Pattala

0 200 400 600 km
0 100 200 300 400 miles

19 The Persian Empire

About 550 B.C. the Persian Cyrus II ascended the throne of the small kingdom of Anshan, defeating Media the same year, then Lydia in 547, and Babylonia in 538. His successor Cambyses II (529-522 B.C.) conquered Egypt. Under Darius I (521-486 B.C.) the empire was divided into satrapies, each headed by a satrap or governor. The fifth satrapy, Abar-Nahara ("[the land] beyond the river [Euphrates]"), included the province of Judah. The Persian empire was gradually weakened by successive rebellions among the satrapies.

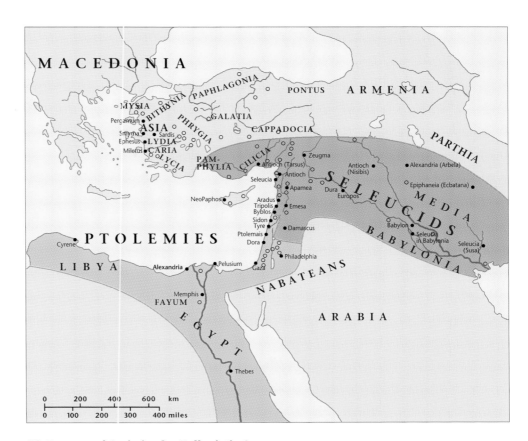

20 Alexander the Great

In the course of the 5th and 4th centuries B.C. the Persian Empire was repeatedly at war with the Greek states. Meanwhile the Greek states were beginning to colonize the coasts of Syria and Palestine and the Nile delta. Greece became united under Philip of Macedon, and when his son Alexander succeeded him as king of Macedonia in 336 B.C., he invaded Asia, defeated the Persian forces in three battles (at Granicus in 334, Issus in 333, and Gaugamela in 331 B.C.), and pressed onward in unprecedented conquests as far as India. In 323 B.C. he died in Babylon, leaving a new and expanded empire to his generals.

21 Egypt and Syria in the Hellenistic Age

After the death of Alexander in 323 B.C. his empire was divided among his generals. Egypt was ruled by Ptolemy and his successors from their capital in Alexandria. Syria was ruled by Seleucus and his successors from Antioch in Syria. Palestine was at first under the Egyptian Ptolemies, but after 198 B.C. it passed to the Syrian Seleucids following the battle of Paneas at the foot of Mount Hermon. Throughout the Near and Middle East the Greeks established new Greek cities and gave older cities new Greek names. The most important of these cities are named on the map, while others are represented by only a circle.

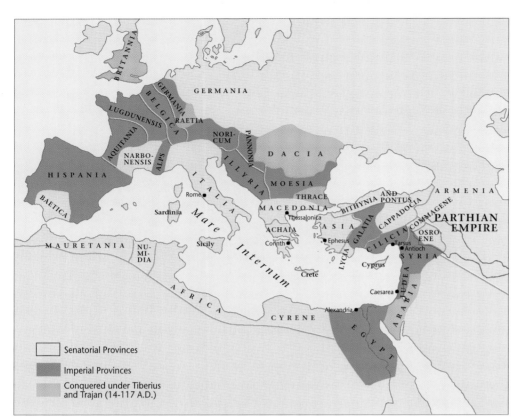

22 The Roman Empire

In 64 B.C. Pompey conquered Syria, and Judea became a Roman province. During the early Imperial period from Augustus to Hadrian (30 B.C.– A.D. 138) the Roman empire achieved its greatest expansion, encompassing the entire civilized world bordering the Mediterranean. The Near East was divided into the provinces of Syria, which included Judea, and Arabia, to the east and south of Judea.

23 The Jewish Diaspora

1 Maccabees 15.10-24 f.; Acts 2.9-11
The Jewish diaspora had its origin in the deportations and waves of refugees of 722 and 598–592 B.C. (cf. map 47). Later the emigration expanded, not only to Babylon and Egypt, but also to Syria, Asia Minor, Greece, and Rome. At the time of Jesus the diaspora numbered some four to five million Jews, while there were only about a half million living in Palestine. Of course many of the diaspora Jews were proselytes. The places mentioned in Acts 2.9-11 are underscored on the map.

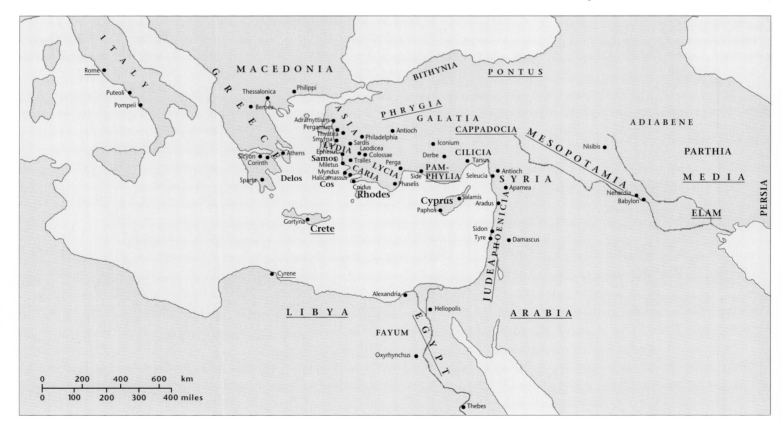

Bible History Maps

The biblical history is not a history written as people today understand the concept of history. Especially in the Old Testament, the accounts sometimes represent the way in which ancient peoples would express and recount the deeper realities of life in a narrative form. Often in the biblical account of an event its meaning for the believing community and their profession of faith are fused together in an indivisible unity. As these accounts are expressions of a religious or theological mystery, they provide in their various forms and fashions a kind of narrative theology. Consequently it is not possible to represent biblical history and secular history in a single series of maps.

The maps in this third part of the *Bible Atlas* are based specifically and exclusively on the biblical texts indicated for each. For example, map 28 "Jacob" illustrates the text of Genesis 27–35: it shows only places that are mentioned in these chapters.

But there are some exceptions. Occasionally non-biblical texts are referred to because they provide significant information about the period under consideration. For example, map 39 "The Kingdoms of Israel and Judah" illustrates the texts of 1 Kings 12–15 and 2 Chronicles 10–15. The map also shows the route of Pharaoh Shishak's invasion as reconstructed from a temple inscription at Karnak in Egypt. Map 42 "The Fall of the Kingdom of Israel" draws on Assyrian texts to describe the political reorganization of areas lost to the Assyrians in 732 B.C. Map 25 "The Biblical Table of Nations" based on the genealogical table in Genesis 10 is matched with map 26 showing a later revision of the genealogical table according to Jubilees 8–9.

Finally it should be mentioned that this part of the *Bible Atlas* contains a few purely historical maps based on non-biblical information (e.g., writings of the first century Jewish historian Josephus), such as map 49 ("Palestine in the Hellenistic Period") and map 52 ("Palestine Reorganized by Pompey"). These maps could have been placed in the second part with the secular historical maps, but thematically they are more convenient here.

Mount Tabor, traditionally the place of the Transfiguration (Mark 9.1-13). Its Old Testament associations are with Deborah and the war with the Canaanite king Jabin of Hazor (Judges 4).

Terebinth Valley in the foothills of Judah on the border between the Philistines and the Israelites. Here tradition places the encounter between David and Goliath (1 Samuel 17). In the background the Judean highlands rise like a fortress.

The Jordan Valley viewed from Pella, toward the Plain of Jezreel. To the left is Mount Gilboa with Beth-shan below. Mount Gilboa was the scene of the battle where Saul and his sons died (1 Samuel 31).

Lake Galilee viewed from the northwest. In the foreground is et-Tabgha, traditionally the site of the Feeding of the 5,000 (Mark 6.30-44) and one of the appearance to the disciples (John 21.1-14).

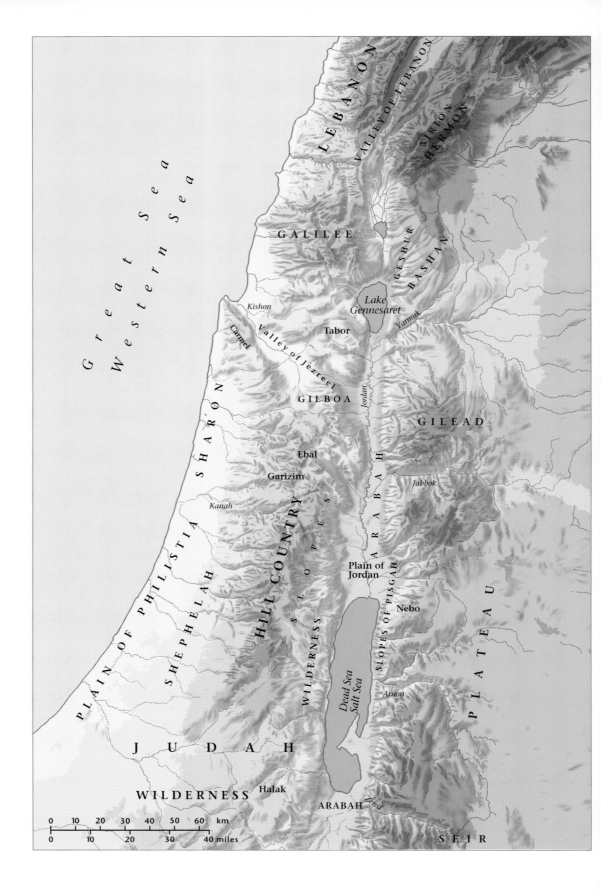

LEBANON

VALLEY OF LEBANON

SIRION
HERMON

G A L I L E E

GESHUR

BASHAN

Great Sea
Western Sea

Lake
Gennesaret

Kishon

Yarmuk

Tabor

Carmel

Valley of Jezreel

GILBOA

GILEAD

SHARON

Jordan

A
R
A
B
A
H

Ebal

Jabbok

Garizim

Kanah

HILL COUNTRY

S
L
O
P
E
S

Plain of
Jordan

Nebo

SLOPES OF PISGAH

SHEPHELAH

WILDERNESS

PLAIN OF PHILISTIA

Armon

Dead Sea
Salt Sea

J U D A H

WILDERNESS   Halak

Zered

ARABAH

| 0 | 10 | 20 | 30 | 40 | 50 | 60 | km |

| 0 | 10 | 20 | 30 | 40 miles |

S E I R

P L A T E A U

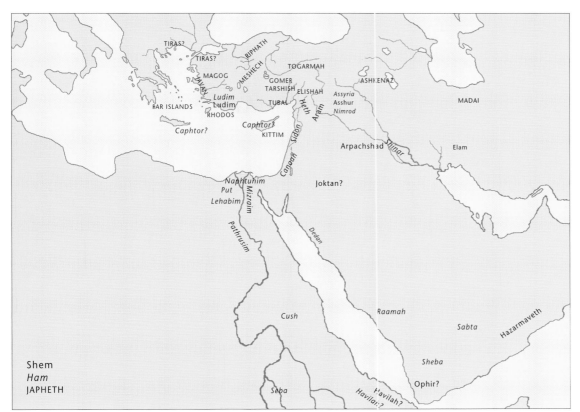

TIRAS?
TIRAS?
RIPHATH
MAGOG
TOGARMAH
JAVAN
MESHECH
GOMER
ASHKENAZ
Ludim
TARSHISH
ELISHAH
MADAI
Ludim
TUBAL
Assyria
BAR ISLANDS
RHODOS
Heth
Asshur
Caphtor?
Aram
Nimrod
Caphtor?
KITTIM
Sidon
Arpachshad
Shinar
Elam
Naphtuhim
Carpach
Put
Joktan?
Lehabim
Mizraim
Pathrusim
Dedan
Cush
Raamah
Sabta
Hazarmaveth
Sheba
Seba
Havilah?
Ophir?
Havilah?
Shem
Ham
JAPHETH

25 The Biblical Table of Nations

Genesis 10
The genealogical table in Genesis 10 reflects Israel's views of world geography in the post-Exilic period. It was probably compiled in the 5th or 4th century B.C., incorporating earlier materials and primitive traditions. The peoples of the world are divided into three groups descended from the three sons of Noah: Shem, Ham and Japheth. Despite the many doublets in the list, it is evident that Shem lives to the east, Ham to the south, and Japheth to the north, corresponding to the three regions of the earth then recognized. The names are represented here on a modern map of the Middle East.

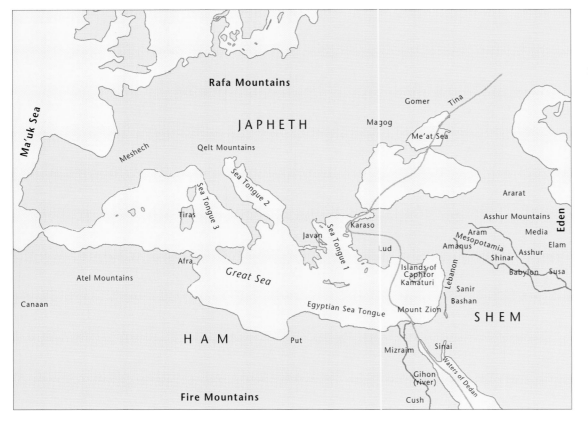

Rafa Mountains
Ma'uk Sea
Gomer
Tina
JAPHETH
Magog
Me'at Sea
Meshech
Qelt Mountains
Ararat
Sea Tongue 2
Asshur Mountains
Tiras
Media
Sea Tongue 3
Aram
Mesopotamia
Elam
Javan
Amanus
Karaso
Sea Tongue 1
Shinar
Asshur
Afra
Lud
Babylon
Susa
Atel Mountains
Great Sea
Islands of
Caphtor
Lebanon
Kamaturi
Sanir
Canaan
Egyptian Sea Tongue
Mount Zion
Bashan
Put
SHEM
HAM
Mizraim
Sinai
Gihon
(river)
Waters of Dedan
Fire Mountains
Cush
Eden

26 The Biblical Table of Nations in the Hellenistic Period

Jubilees 8–9
The book of Jubilees from the 2nd century B.C. presents a revised form of the table of nations in Genesis 10, interpreting it in the light of the new geographical knowledge of the Hellenistic period. It tells how the world was allotted to the three sons of Noah. Shem received the best part, the central part of the earth bounded by a line extending northward to the Tina (Don) River through Karaso (Hellespont) and the Caspian and Me'at (Azov) seas, and southward from Karaso through Lud to the waters of Dedan (Red Sea). All the lands north and west of this line belonged to Japheth, and the lands south and west were the heritage of Ham.

27 Abraham and Isaac

Genesis 11.27–25.18
Abraham was from Ur Kasdim, or Ur of the Chaldees, going first to Haran in Upper Mesopotamia and then on to Canaan, where he settled in Hebron. Through Isaac, his son by Sarah, he became the ancestor of all the Israelite tribes. Through Ishmael, his son by Hagar, and other sons by other wives, he became the ancestor of other nations.

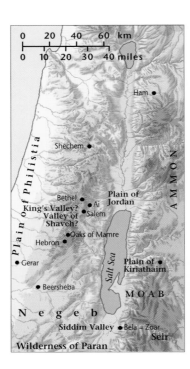

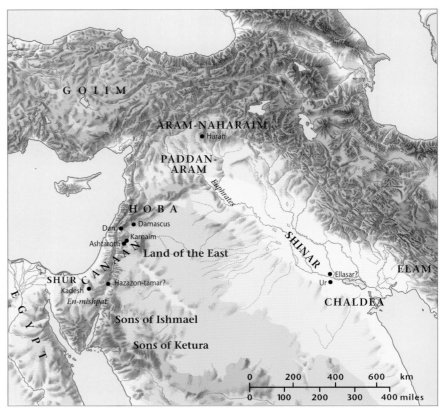

28 Jacob

Genesis 27–35
The traditions about Jacob, who is also identified as Israel in Genesis 32.28 and 35.10, reflect traditions of the northern kingdom, suggesting a possible association with the Arameans (cf. map 16), or with the deportees in Mesopotamia (cf. map 47).

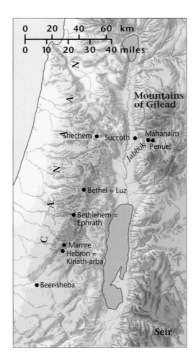

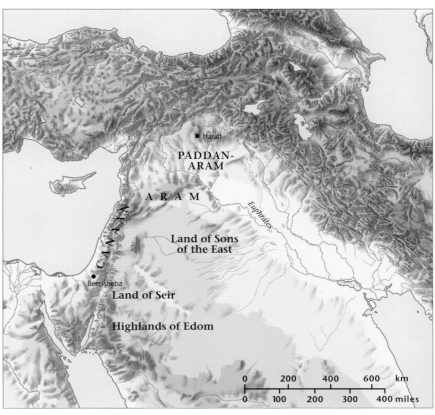

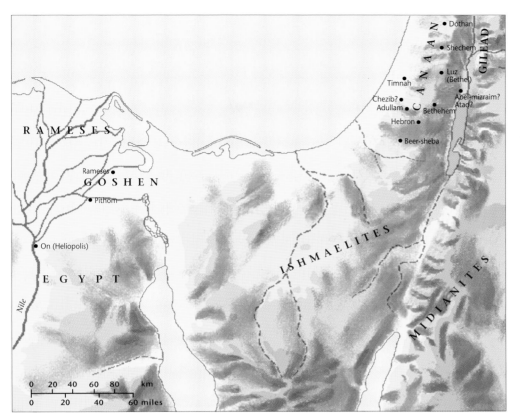

29 The Story of Joseph: Israel in Egypt

Genesis 37–Exodus 1
The story of Joseph in its present form dates from late in the period of the monarchy. It links the patriarchal period, and its traditions of wandering and settlement in Canaan, with the traditions of the exodus from Egypt, the wanderings in the desert, and the conquest of Canaan under Joshua's leadership.

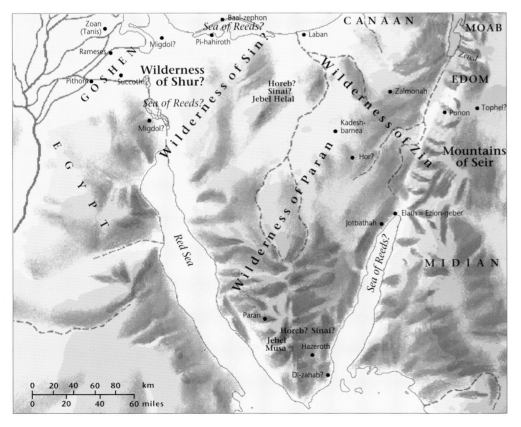

30 The Exodus from Egypt and Wanderings in the Desert

Exodus 12.37–19.2; Numbers 10.11f; 12.16; 14; 20; 33; Deuteronomy 1–2
Many of the places named in the traditions about the exodus from Egypt and the desert wanderings cannot be identified with any certainty. Only those which are known with a reasonable degree of certainty are shown on the map. See also map 31, as the traditions about the desert wanderings and settlement in the Transjordan are closely interwoven.

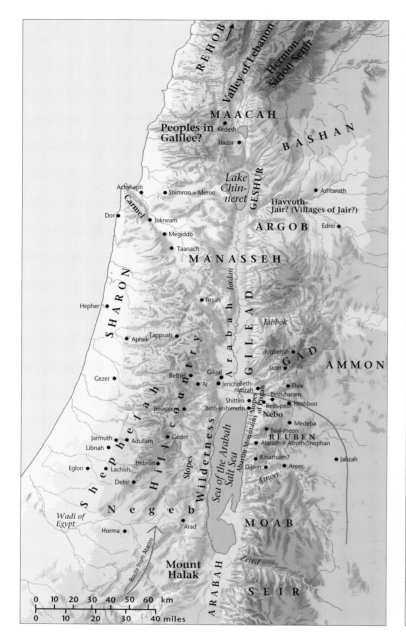

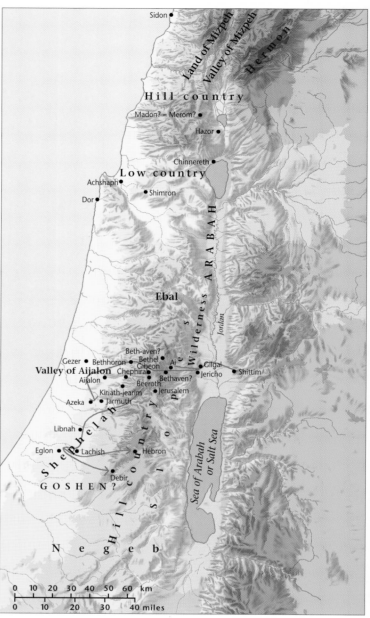

31 The Conquest of Canaan

Numbers 13–14; 21–32; Deuteronomy 2–3; Joshua 12
The map is based on three distinct traditions which were eventually combined in a single narrative. The mission of the spies in Numbers 13–14 reflects an immigration into Canaan from the south. The conquest of Transjordan is recounted in Numbers 21–32 and Deuteronomy 2–3. The conquest of Canaan is finally summarized in Joshua 12 by a list of conquered lands and cities. These three traditions account for all the territory of Palestine and the southern Transjordan later claimed by Israel.

32 The Conquest by Joshua

Joshua 2.1–11.15
The account of Joshua's conquest deals with only two areas in the promised land. The first campaign was in the south, concentrating primarily in the area later occupied by the tribe of Benjamin, and with the Israelites' base camp at Gilgal near the Jordan (Joshua 2–10). The second campaign was the conquest of Galilee at the battle of Merom Waters and the capture of Hazor, the chief city of the region (Joshua 11.1-15). No mention is made of the central hill country (cf. the lists in Joshua 13–19 and map 33).

33 The Division of the Land

Joshua 13–19. See map 44 for Joshua 15.20-62; 18.21-28; 19.40-46

After Joshua's conquest, the land was divided among the tribes of Israel. The lists in Joshua 13–19 contain diverse elements. Some describe boundaries while others are lists of cities. Dating the lists is difficult because they reflect different periods in the history of Israel. One of the lists (Joshua 15.20-62, the cities of Judah) is generally assigned to the reign of King Josiah (cf. map 44). The final composition of Joshua 13–19 was evidently during the Hasmonean period, reflecting their territorial claims (cf. map 51).

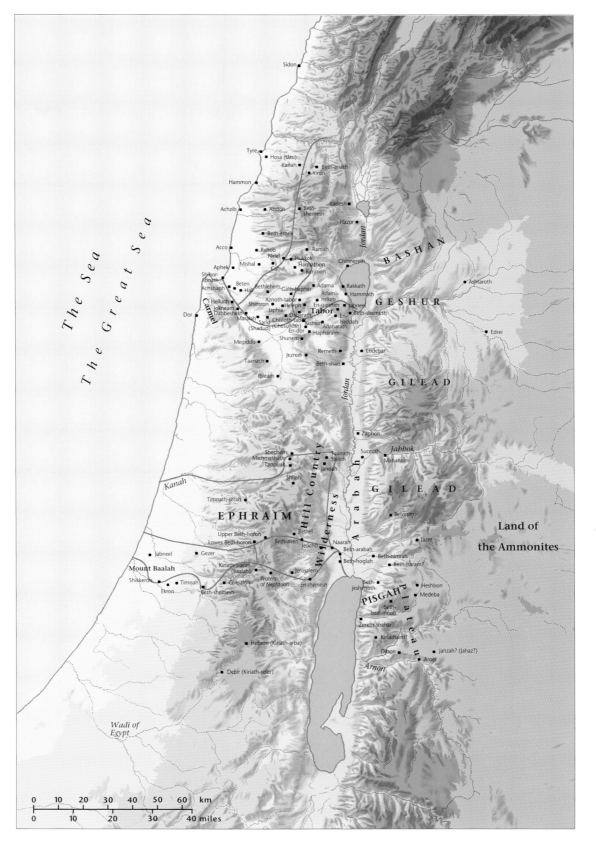

34 The Levitical Cities

*Joshua 21; 1 Chronicles 6.39-66
(Vulgate 6.54-81)*
When the land of Palestine was divided among the tribes of Israel the clans of the priestly tribe of Levi were not allotted a single area for their settlement. Instead they were given certain cities within the areas allotted to the other tribes. A number of these cities were also designated places of refuge, where a person accused of accidental killing could find sanctuary from avengers.

The origins of this list are unknown.

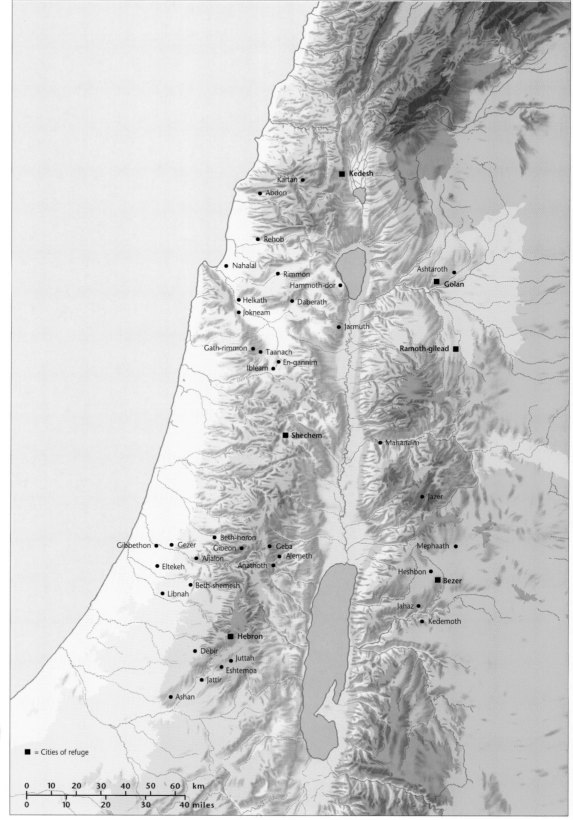

Kartan
■ Kedesh
Abdon

Rehob

Nahalal
Rimmon
Ashtaroth
Hammoth-dor
■ Golan
Helkath
Daberath
Jokneam
Jarmuth
Gath-rimmon
Ramoth-gilead ■
Taanach
Ibleam
En-gannim

■ Shechem
Mahanaim

Jazer

Beth-horon
Gibbethon Gezer
Mephaath
Gibeon
Geba
Ajalon
Alemeth
Eltekeh
Anathoth
Heshbon
Bezer ■
Beth-shemesh
Libnah
Jahaz
Kedemoth

■ Hebron
Debir
Juttah
Eshtemoa
Jattir
Ashan

■ = Cities of refuge

| 0 | 10 | 20 | 30 | 40 | 50 | 60 | km |
| 0 | 10 | 20 | 30 | 40 miles |

35 The Period of the Judges

Judges 1–21; 1 Samuel 1–7
The time between the conquest of Palestine and the reign of King Saul is called the period of the judges. Judges 1–21 and 1 Samuel 1–7 preserve the traditions of various tribes and clans from this period as they were later edited to form a continuous narrative. It is almost impossible to determine the chronological and historical relationships of these traditions to each other and assign them precise dates.

In the archaeology of Palestine this is the early Iron Age, approximately between 1200 and 1000 B.C. The map shows the extent to which the Israelites were able to occupy the land of Canaan, and the areas and cities they were unable to conquer (Judges 1.27-36).

To Hamath

SIDONIANS
Sidon
Mahalab = Ahlab
Beth-anath
HAROSHETH-HA-GOIIM?
Achzib
Beth-shemesh
Acco
Rehob
ASHER
Arumah
ZEBULUN
Dor
Tabor
Ophrah
ISSACHAR
Megiddo
Hill of Moreh
Taanach
Spring of Harod
Beth-shan
Ibleam
MACHIR

LEBANON
Lebanon
BETH-REHOB
Hermon
ARAM
Laish = Dan
DAN
NAPHTALI
Hazor
Kishon
Valley of Jezreel
Kedesh
TOB
Kamon?
Havvoth-jair? (Villages of Jair?)
Tabbath?
MANASSEH
Jabesh
Abel-mehola
Bezek
MACHIR
Shamir? = Samaria
Thebez? = Tirzah
Jabbok
MANASSEH
Garizim
Shechem
Succoth
Pirathon
Penuel
Jordan
Zeredah = Zarethan
Aphik = Aphek
Ramathaim
EPHRAIM
LEBONAH
Shiloh
GILEAD
Timnath-heres = Timnath-serah
Jeshanah
BENJAMIN
Wilderness
Jogbehah
Rabbah
AMMON
Shaalbim
Bethel = Luz
Gilgal
Gezer
Aijalon
Mizpah
Ramah
City of Palms? = Jericho
Gibea
Geba
Abel-keramim?
Valley of Sorek
Kiriathjearim
To Karkor
Ashdod
Timnah
Eshtaol
Jerusalem
Heshbon
Ekron
Zorah
Beth-shemesh
Bethlehem
Gath
Shephelah
Etam
REUBEN
Ashkelon
GAD
Gaza
Hebron = Kiriath-arba
Jahzah (Jahaz)
JUDAH
Aroer
Debir = Kiriath-sepher
Arnon
PHILISTINES
Negeb
MOAB
Zephath (Horma)
Arad
Beer-sheba
SIMEON
To Kadesh-barnea
Sons of the East

0 10 20 30 40 50 60 km
0   10   20   30   40 miles
Ascent of Akrabbim
AMALEKITES City of Palms? = Tamar
SEIR EDOM
Sela?

36 Saul

1 Samuel 9–31; 2 Samuel 2.8f;
1 Chronicles 9.35–10.14

In response to external pressures, especially from the Philistines, the leader Saul from the tribe of Benjamin succeeded about 1000 B.C. in uniting the tribes and clans of Israel as a kingdom, or rather a chiefdom, although he was unable to establish their territorial integrity. His reign was characterized externally by wars and internally by his rivalry with David. Saul was killed together with his sons in battle against the Philistines on Mount Gilboa, probably in an attempt to join together the territories of the central and northern Israelite tribes.

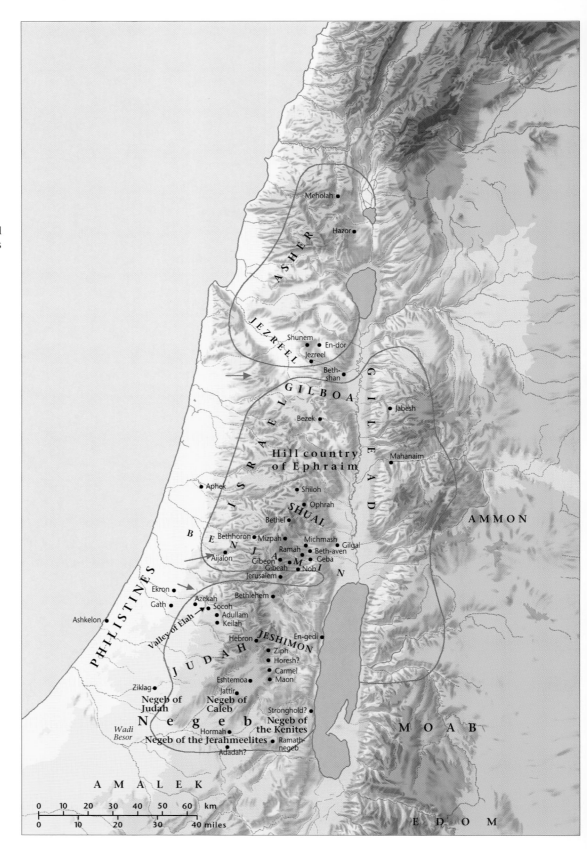

Meholah

Hazor

ASHER

JEZREEL

Shunem
En-dor
Jezreel
Beth-shan

GILBOA

GILEAD

Jabesh

Bezek

Mahanaim

Hill country
of Ephraim

AMMON

Aphek
Shiloh
Ophrah

SHUAL

Bethel

BENJAMIN
Bethhoron
Mizpah
Michmash
Ramah   Beth-aven
Gilgal
Aijalon
Gibeon
Geba
Gibeah
Nob
Jerusalem

Ekron
Bethlehem

Gath
Azekah
Socoh
Adullam
Keilah

Ashkelon

PHILISTINES

Valley of Elah

Hebron   JESHIMON
En-gedi
Ziph
Horesh?
Carmel
Maon

JUDAH

Eshtemoa

Ziklag
Jattir
Negeb of
Judah
Negeb of
Caleb
Stronghold?

N e g e b
Negeb of
the Kenites

MOAB

Wadi
Besor
Hormah
Negeb of the Jerahmeelites   Ramath-
negeb
Adadah?

AMALEK

| 0 | 10 | 20 | 30 | 40 | 50 | 60 | km |

| 0 | 10 | 20 | 30 | 40 miles |

EDOM

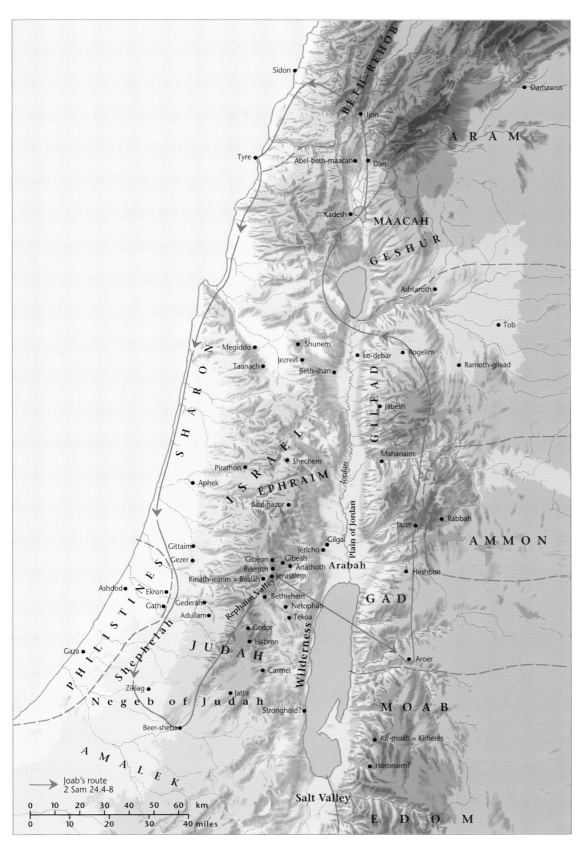

37 David

2 Samuel 2–1 Kings 2; 1 Chronicles 11–29
David was first anointed king of Judah in Hebron, and then also king of Israel after the death of Ishbosheth. He conquered the Jebusite city of Jerusalem and made it his capital. He then proceeded to capture several Canaanite cities in the north (Megiddo, Taanach, Beth-shan), and in the following years subjugated the kingdoms of Edom, Moab and Ammon. Apparently the Philistines in Damascus and Aram were vassals.

In 2 Samuel 24 there is the account of a census commissioned by David and undertaken by Joab. The itinerary followed by Joab in 2 Samuel 24.5-8 presents an ideal outline of the extent of David's kingdom.

Map labels

Sidon · Damascus · BETH-REHOB · Ijon · ARAM · Tyre · Abel-beth-maacah · Dan · Kadesh · MAACAH · GESHUR · Ashtaroth · Tob · Megiddo · Shunem · Lo-debar · Rogelim · Taanach · Jezreel · Beth-shan · Ramoth-gilead · GILEAD · Jabesh · SHARON · ISRAEL · Mahanaim · Pirathon · Shechem · EPHRAIM · Aphek · Baal-hazor · Jazer · Rabbah · AMMON · Gittaim · Gilgal · Jericho · Plain of Jordan · Gezer · Gibeon · Gibeah · Jordan · Beeroth · Anathoth · Arabah · Kiriath-jearim = Baalah · Jerusalem · Heshbon · Ashdod · Ekron · Bethlehem · Gath · Gederah · Netophah · GAD · Adullam · Tekoa · Rephaim Valley · Gedor · Gaza · Hebron · Wilderness · Carmel · Aroer · JUDAH · Ziklag · Jattir · MOAB · Stronghold? · Beer-sheba · Kir-moab = Kirheres · AMALEK · Negeb of Judah · Shephelah · PHILISTINES · Horonaim? · Salt Valley · EDOM

→ Joab's route 2 Sam 24.4-8

| 0 | 10 | 20 | 30 | 40 | 50 | 60 | km |

| 0 | 10 | 20 | 30 | 40 miles |

---

38 Solomon

1 Kings 1–12; 2 Chronicles 1-9
Solomon's empire extended far beyond the borders of Israel. His vassal states included Aram, Ammon, Moab and Edom, and his commercial ventures expanded throughout the known world. He organized his administration effectively, dividing Israel into twelve provinces based on the traditional tribal boundaries, with a governor for each province.

The map shows the twelve provinces as described in 1 Kings 4, and the cities he fortified as an inner line of defense (1 Kings 9). Finally, it was Solomon who built the Jerusalem temple (cf. map 73).

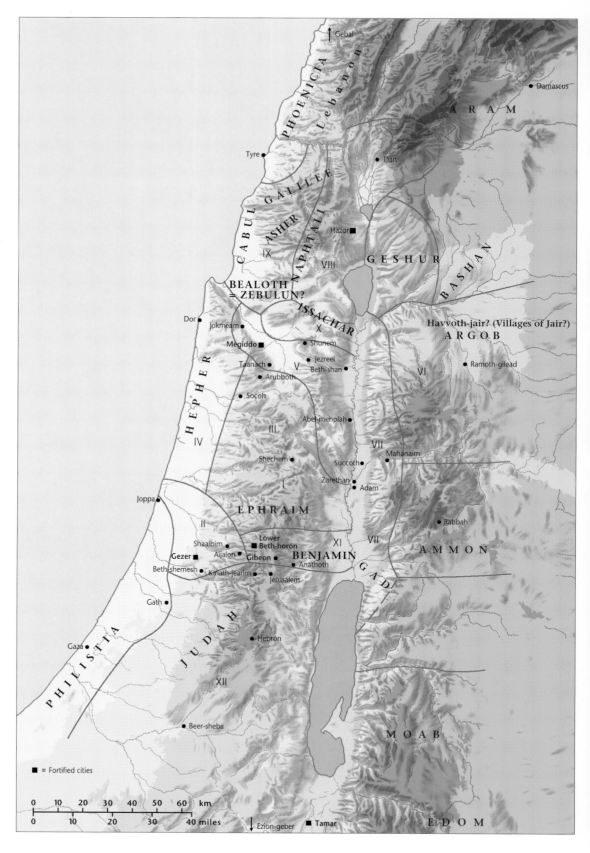

■ = Fortified cities

39 The Kingdoms of Israel and Judah

1 Kings 12–15; 2 Chronicles 10–15

After Solomon's death, Israel divided into two kingdoms: Judah in the south with Jerusalem as its capital; and Israel in the north with its capital at first at Shechem, then Tirzah, and finally at Samaria. King Jeroboam built his own temples at Bethel and at Dan. Only after prolonged combat was the border established with Benjamin as part of Judah.

Shortly after the division Pharaoh Shishak launched an invasion of Israel and Judah. King Rehoboam responded by fortifying a number of cities in Judah.

The map shows the border between the kingdoms, the route of Shishak's invasion (according to the list of conquered cities recorded in the temple at Karnak), and the cities fortified by Rehoboam.

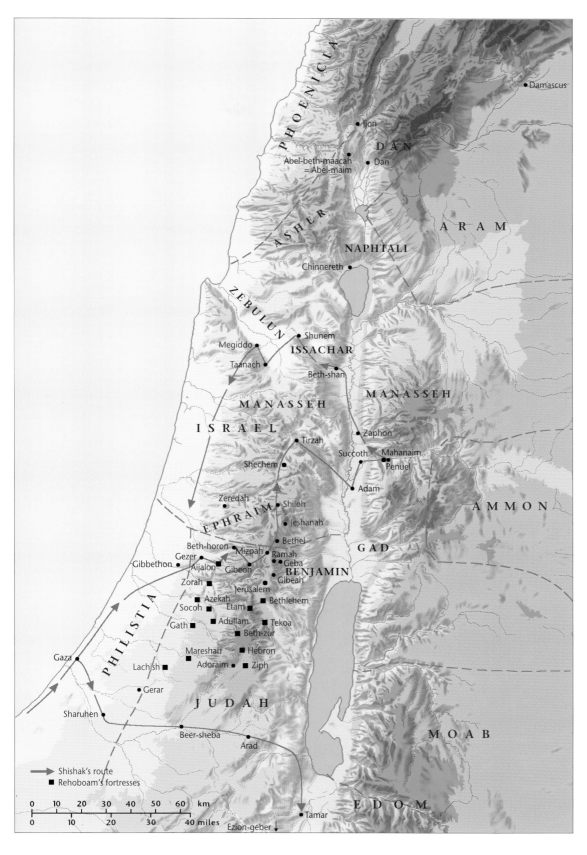

Key:
→ Shishak's route
■ Rehoboam's fortresses

Scale:
0 10 20 30 40 50 60 km
0 10 20 30 40 miles

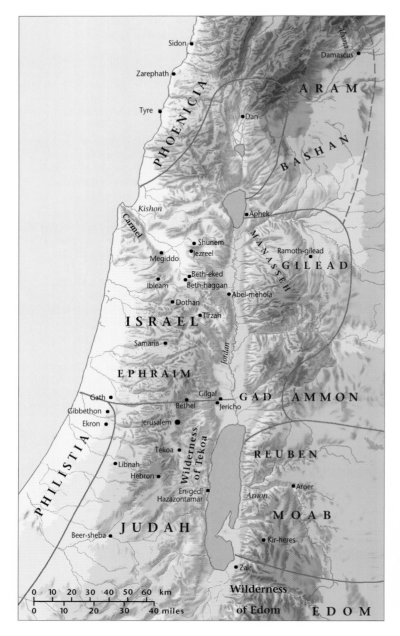

40 The Golden Age of the 9th Century B.C.

1 Kings 16.23–2 Kings 13; 2 Chronicles 17–24
In the mid 9th century B.C., King Omri of Israel and his successor Ahab, with the aid of King Jehoshaphat of Judah, created an empire comparable to that of David and Solomon. Meanwhile King Mesha of Moab was seeking to expand his power westward across the Jordan. Political and religious tensions in Israel led to Jehu's rebellion in 841 B.C., with the destruction of the royal houses of both Israel and Judah and the decline of both kingdoms. This was the period of the prophets Elijah and Elisha in the northern kingdom.

41 The Golden Age of the 8th Century B.C.

2 Kings 13.10–15.7; 2 Chronicles 25–26; Amos
During the period of 790–750 B.C. the kingdom of Israel under Jeroboam II and the kingdom of Judah under Azariah/Uzziah enjoyed a renaissance of power. Both kings were successful in their wars against Syria in the north, and against Ammon, Moab, Edom and the Philistines in the south. They broadly expanded the areas under their authority and gained control over the major caravan routes — a success made possible by the weakened state of the Assyrian empire. This was the period of the prophets Amos of Tekoa and Hosea in the north.

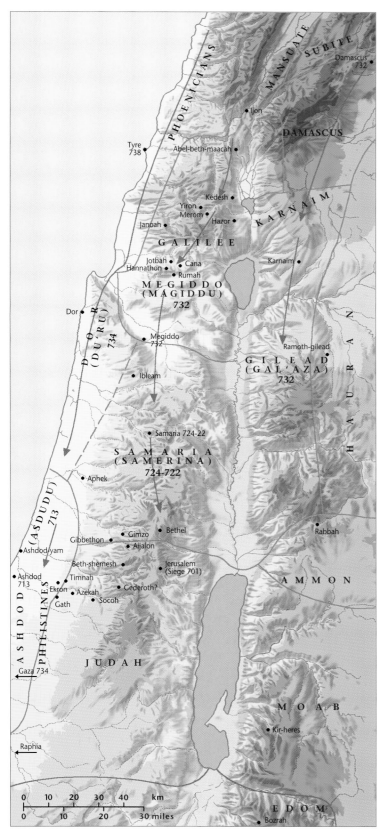

42 The Fall of the Kingdom of Israel

2 Kings 15–17; 2 Chronicles 28.16-21; Isaiah 7–9; 10.28-32; 20
The Assyrian conquests after 750 B.C. led to the fall of the northern kingdom of Israel. In 732 Tiglath-Pileser III (744-727 B.C.) established Dor (Duru), Megiddo (Magiddu) and Gilead (Galaza) as Assyrian provinces, and made Israel and Judah vassal states. Israel rebelled and was defeated by Shalmaneser V (727-722 B.C.), and had its capital Samaria destroyed (722 B.C.). Sargon II (722-705) deported part of the population to Assyria, and made the northern kingdom the province of Samarina (Samaria). In 713 B.C. Sargon conquered the Philistine cities in the south and organized them as the Assyrian province of Asdudu (Ashdod), leaving the kingdom of Judah surrounded by Assyrian provinces (cf. map 17).

43 Judah under King Hezekiah

2 Kings 18–20; 1 Chronicles 4.35-43; 2 Chronicles 29–32;
Isaiah 10.28-32; 20; 36–39; Micah 1.8-16
Under Hezekiah (716-687 B.C.) Judah was a vassal of Assyria. Hezekiah attempted to strengthen his national defenses by designating four cities as military depots. On the death of Sargon II (705 B.C.) Hezekiah rebelled against his successor Sennacherib (704-681 B.C.) who responded in 701 by invading Judah and besieging Jerusalem. Sennacherib defeated an Egyptian force at Eltekeh and made his headquarters in Lachish, the capture of which is depicted on the gates of his new palace in Nineveh.

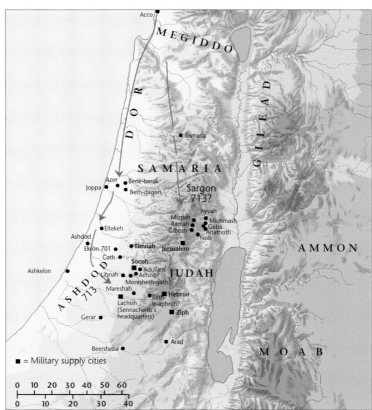

■ = Military supply cities

39

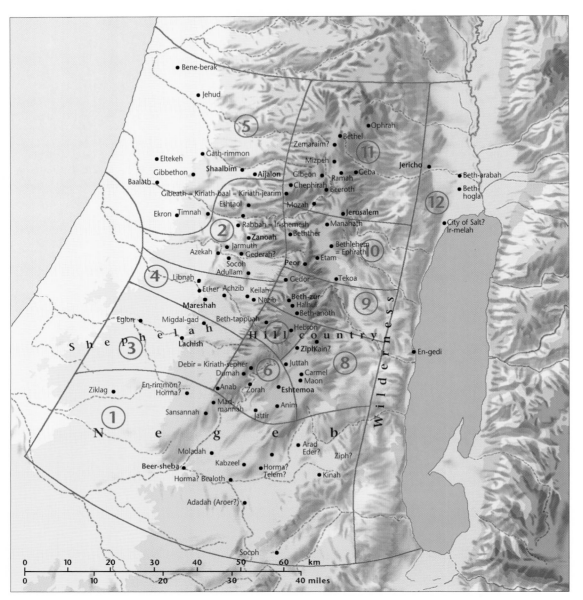

44 The Districts of Judah under King Josiah

Joshua 15.20-62; 18.21-28; 19.40-46

These lists enumerate the towns in the twelve districts of Judah. According to recent scholarship they reflect conditions during the reign of Josiah about 620 B.C., although they are cited in the book of Joshua to illustrate a much earlier period (cf. the notes on map 33). The map shows the districts of Judah and the relative density of their population in the time of Josiah. Only the towns whose locations have been identified are shown on the map. The remainder are listed below it. When the topographical evidence has been convincing, some places have been transposed from the districts indicated in the book of Joshua.

(1)
Jagur
Dimonah
Kedesh
Hazor
Ithnan
Hazor-
  hadatta
Amam
Kerioth-
  hezron
Shema
Hazar-gadda
Heshmon
Beth-pelet
Hazar-
  shual
Baalah
Iim
Ezem
Eltolad
Chesil
Bethul
Lebaoth
Shilhim

(2)
Ashnah
En-gannim
Tappuah
Enam
Shaaraim
Adithaim
Gederothaim

(3)
Zenan
Hadashah
Dilan
Mizpeh
Jokthe-el
Bozkath
Cabbon
Lahmam
Chitlish
Gederoth
Beth-dagon
Naamah
Makkedah

(4)
Ashan
Iphtah
Ashnah

(5)
Ithla
Elon
Me-jarkon
Rakkon

(6)
Shamir
Dannah
Goshen
Holon
Giloh

(7)
Arab
Eshan
Janim (Janum)
Aphekah
Humtah
Zior

(8)
Jezreel
Jokdeam
Zanoah
Gibeah
Timnah

(9)
Maarath
Eltekon

(10)
Kulon
Tatam
Shoresh
Kerem
Gallim

(11)
Avim
Parah
Chefar-
  ammoni
Ophni
Rekem
Irpeel
Taralah
Zela
Haeleph

(12)
Emek-keziz
Middin
Secacah
Nibshan

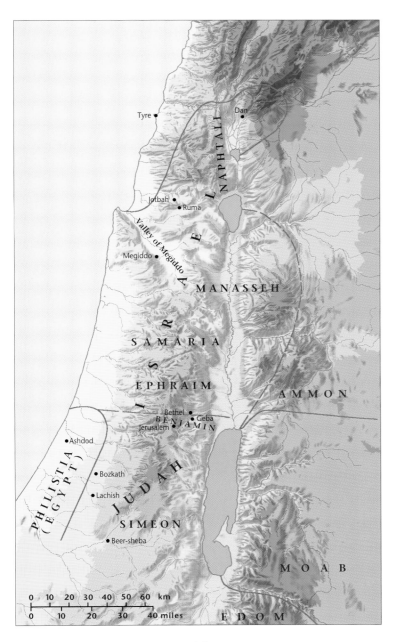

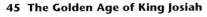

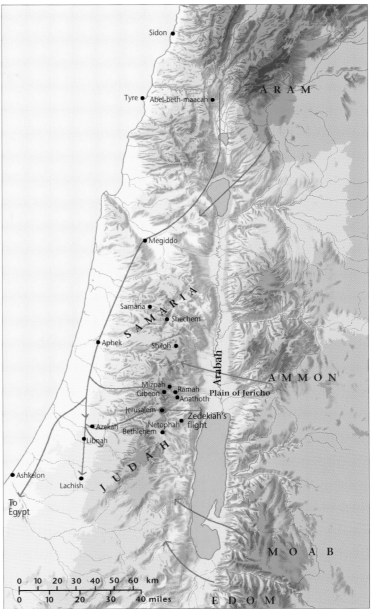

45 The Golden Age of King Josiah

2 Kings 21–23; 2 Chronicles 33–35

As the Assyrian empire weakened (cf. map 17), Josiah was able to recapture parts of Israel that had been lost in 732 and 722 B.C. However, the extent to which he established his control over the former northern kingdom is questionable. Josiah was killed at Megiddo in an attempt to halt an Egyptian army from joining forces to support the Assyrian army in its frontier wars (cf. map 18). Josiah's reign saw the beginning of Jeremiah's prophetic ministry.

46 The Fall of Judah

2 Kings 24–25; 2 Chronicles 36; Jeremiah 27.3; 32; 37–39; 52

The Neo-Babylonian King Nebuchadnezzar (605–562 B.C.) responded to revolts by Judah in 597, 587 and 582 B.C. with attacks and deportations. In 587 Jerusalem was destroyed. King Zedekiah fled toward the Jordan, but was captured and taken north to Riblah and then to Babylon. Judah became a Babylonian province with its capital at Mizpah. The Babylonian campaign made use of contingents from Aram, Ammon, Moab and Edom, and after the campaign Edomites settled in southern Judah.

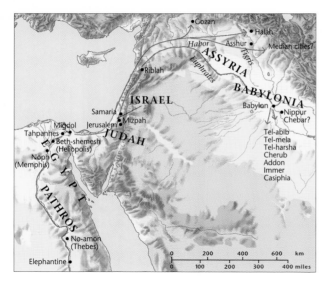

47 Exile in Assyria, Babylon and Egypt

*2 Kings 17.6; 18.11; 24.11-16; 25; Ezra 2.59; 8.17;
Nehemiah 7.61; Jeremiah 29; 42–46; 52; Ezekiel 1.1-3; 3.15*
The exile, marking the beginning of the Jewish diaspora,
resulted from the deportations of the northern kingdom
of Israel to Assyria in 722 B.C., the southern kingdom of
Judah to Babylon in 597, 587 and 582 B.C., and the
flight of many of the remaining population of Judah to
Egypt after an unsuccessful uprising against the Babylonian governor in Mizpah in 582 B.C.

48 Palestine in the Post-Exilic Period

Ezra 2.21-35; Nehemiah 3.1-32; 7.26-38
When the Persian king Cyrus II (550-529 B.C.) conquered Babylon in 539 B.C. with hardly a battle, Judah
became the Persian province Yahud.

The whole of Palestine was part of the 5th Persian
satrapy of Abar-Nahara ("[the land] beyond the
[Euphrates] River"); cf. map 19. The satrapy was divided
into provinces, two of which were Samaria and Yahud.
The capital of Samaria was Shechem, with the holy
mountain of Gerizim. In Nehemiah's time the governor
of Samaria was Sanballat, and the governor of Ammon
was Tobiah. Both governors together with the provinces
of Ashdod and Edom were opposed to Nehemiah and his
plans to rebuild the walls of Jerusalem.

There is a list of Jewish cities in Nehemiah 11.25-35,
but it probably reflects a different period, possibly
including places where the inhabitants escaped deporta-
tion in 587 B.C. The places Lod, Hadid and Ono which
are mentioned in Ezra 2.33 and Nehemiah 7.37 must
have been outside the province of Yahud.

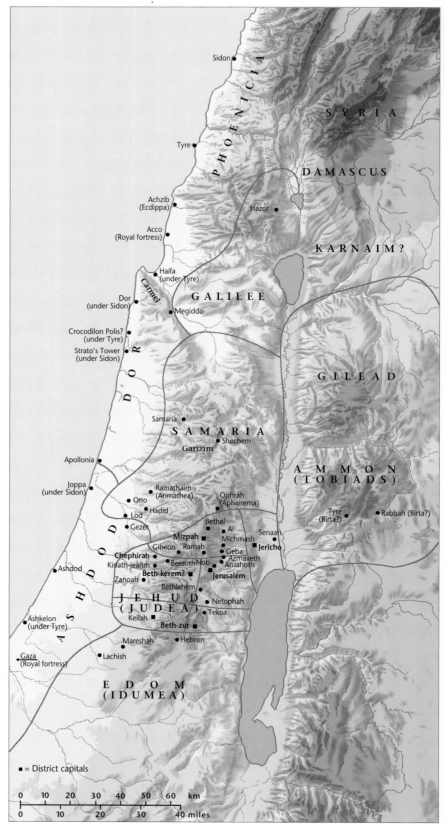

■ = District capitals

49 Palestine in the Hellenistic Period

When Alexander the Great died in 323 B.C., Palestine came under the control of the Ptolemaic kings of Egypt (cf. map 21). They preserved the Persian provinces but divided them into smaller units. They also conferred on a number of towns the status of Greek cities with certain privileges, such as the right to mint their own coins.

After several wars which lasted nearly a century and were known as the Syrian wars, Antiochus III of Syria (223-187 B.C.) defeated the Egyptian forces at the battle of Paneas (198 B.C.), and Phoenicia and Palestine passed under Syrian control with the name Coelesyria. The map shows the administrative divisions in the 2nd century B.C.

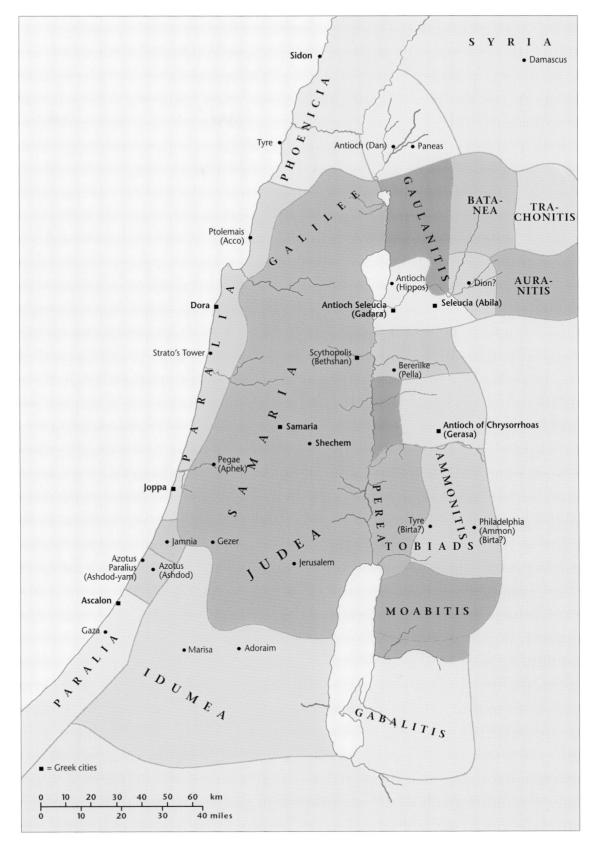

■ = Greek cities

```
0   10  20  30  40  50  60  km
0      10      20      30      40 miles
```

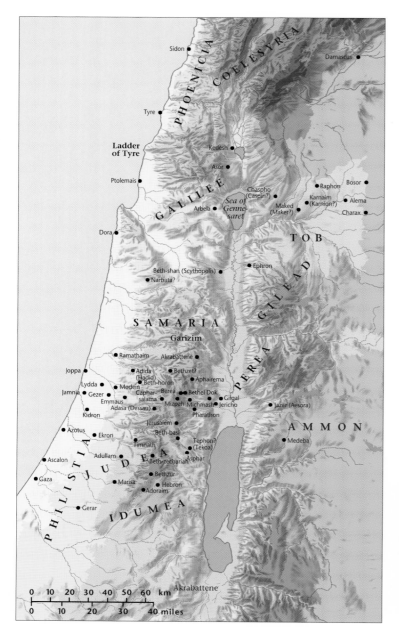

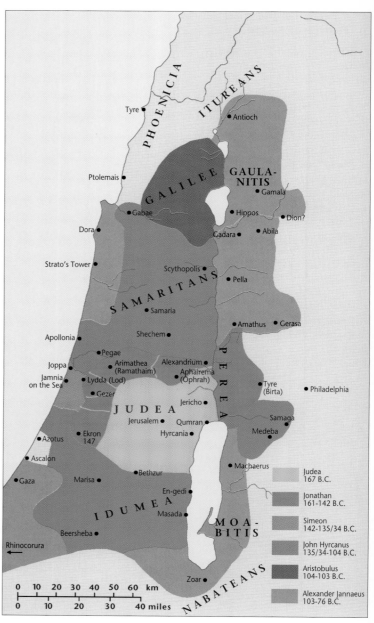

50 The Maccabees

1-2 Maccabees

In 168 B.C. Antiochus IV Epiphanes (175-164 B.C.) set up an altar to Zeus in the temple at Jerusalem. This led to a Jewish uprising under the leadership of the priest Mattathias of Modein and his five sons, the most prominent of whom was Judas Maccabaeus from whom the movement took its name. After more than two decades of fighting Judea achieved independence as a kingdom under Syrian rule. Its royal dynasty was known as Hasmonean after Hasmon, the grandfather of Mattathias.

51 Alexander Jannaeus

While Syria was weakened by civil wars and finally overpowered by Rome, the Jews were able to expand their territory at the expense of their neighboring nations and subjugate the free Greek cities. Under Alexander Jannaeus (103-76 B.C.) the country was comparable to the area of Israel and Judah in the period of the kings.

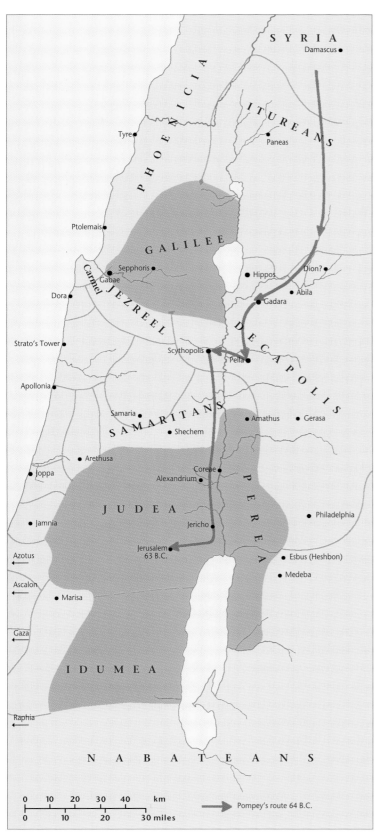

52 Palestine Reorganized by Pompey

When Pompey was in Syria in 64 B.C., he intervened in the civil war between the brothers Hyrcanus II and Aristobulus II. He occupied Palestine and restored the freedom of the Greek cities. He confirmed Hyrcanus as High Priest (not as king) of Judea, Galilee, Perea and eastern Idumea. But the real political power lay in the hands of Antipater, an Idumean, who was appointed procurator of Palestine by Caesar in 47 B.C.

53 The Decapolis

After Pompey's conquest of Palestine, a group of Greek cities joined in forming a league known as the Decapolis (Greek, "Ten Cities"). The league was under the direct authority of the Roman governor of Syria. The membership of the league was not precisely defined: at one point even Damascus was a member. After A.D. 106 the two southernmost cities of Gerasa and Philadelphia belonged to the province of Arabia, and the league was dissolved. Archaeologically all the cities of the Decapolis are characterized by significant remains from the Hellenistic-Roman period.

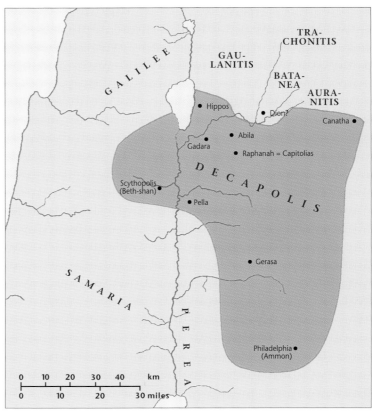

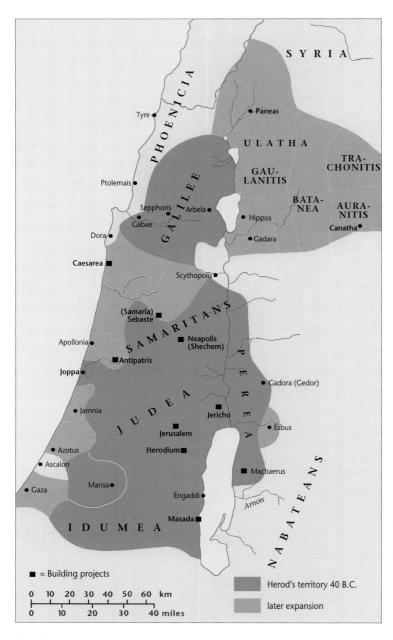

■ = Building projects

0 10 20 30 40 50 60 km
0 10 20 30 40 miles

Herod's territory 40 B.C.

later expansion

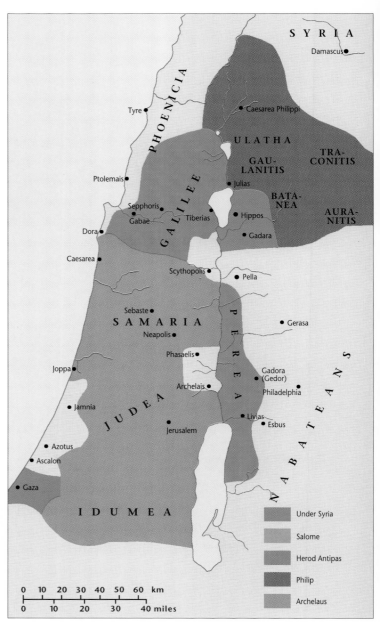

0 10 20 30 40 50 60 km
0 10 20 30 40 miles

Under Syria

Salome

Herod Antipas

Philip

Archelaus

54 Herod

After the assassination of Caesar in 44 B.C. Palestine was also plagued by civil wars. Herod, the son of Antipater, became king of the Jews in 44 B.C., but he did not take Jerusalem until 37 B.C. He continued to extend his authority until the country was the largest it had been since the reign of Solomon. As a builder he was also comparable to Solomon: he transformed the Jerusalem temple into a magnificent Hellenistic-Roman style monument.

55 Herod's Successors

On Herod's death in 4 B.C. Augustus divided his kingdom among his three surviving sons. Archelaus became ethnarch of Judea, Idumea and Samaria. Herod Antipas became tetrarch of Galilee and Perea. Philip became tetrarch of Auranitis, Batanea, Gaulanitis, Trachonitis and Ulatha. Salome, the sister of Herod, was given Jamnia and Azotus on the coast, as well as Phasaelis in the Jordan valley. Archelaus was exiled in A.D. 6, and his territory was administered by a Roman procurator.

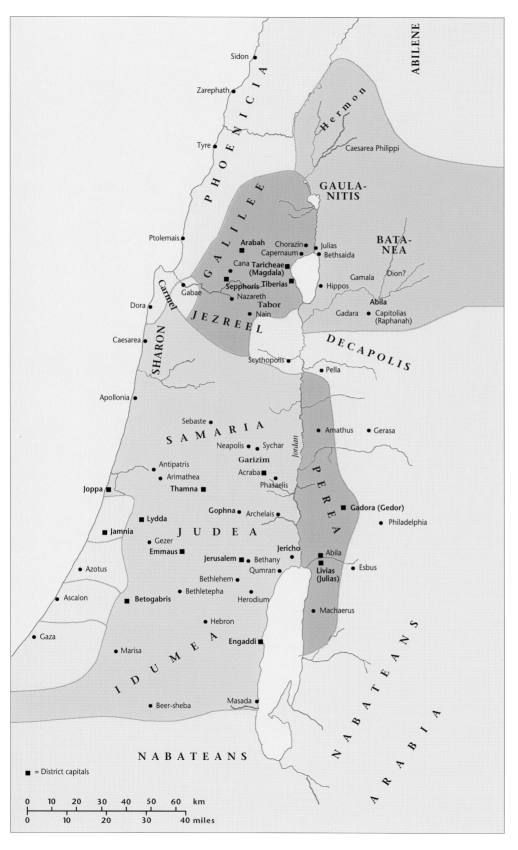

56 Palestine in the Time of Jesus

Idumea, Judea and Samaria were administered by a Roman prefect resident in Caesarea who bore the title procurator after A.D. 41. Herod Antipas was tetrarch of Galilee and Perea, and Philip was tetrarch of Gaulanitis and Batanea, lands to the northeast and east of Lake Galilee. The cities of the Decapolis (cf. map 53) were under the direct control of the governor of Syria.

Map labels:

ABILENE

Sidon

Zarephath

PHOENICIA

Hermon

Tyre

Caesarea Philippi

GALILEE

GAULA-NITIS

Ptolemais

Arabah Chorazin Julias
Capernaum Bethsaida

BATA-NEA

Cana Taricheae (Magdala)

Gamala Dion?

Sepphoris Tiberias

Gabae Nazareth

Dora

Carmel

Hippos

JEZREEL Tabor Nain

Abila

Gadara Capitolias (Raphanah)

Caesarea

SHARON

DECAPOLIS

Scythopolis

Pella

Apollonia

Sebaste

SAMARIA

Amathus Gerasa

Neapolis Sychar

Jordan

Garizim

Antipatris Acraba

Arimathea Phasaelis

PEREA

Joppa Thamna

Gophna Archelais

Gadora (Gedor)

Lydda

Philadelphia

Jamnia

Gezer

JUDEA

Emmaus Jericho Abila

Jerusalem Bethany

Livias (Julias) Esbus

Azotus

Qumran

Bethlehem

Ascalon

Bethletepha Herodium

Machaerus

Betogabris

NABATEANS

Hebron

Gaza

Marisa

IDUMEA

Engaddi

Beer-sheba Masada

NABATEANS

ARABIA

■ = District capitals

0 10 20 30 40 50 60 km

0 10 20 30 40 miles

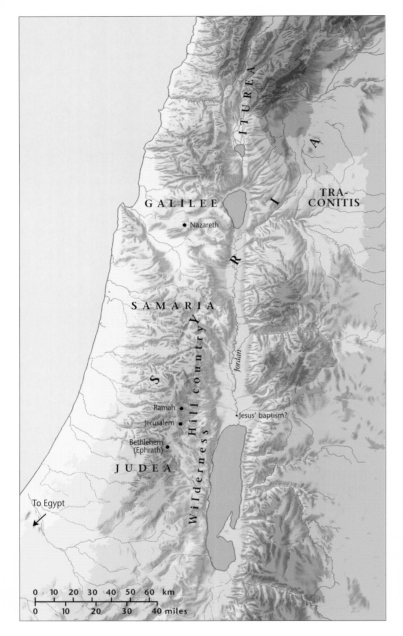

57 The Birth, Childhood and Baptism of Jesus

Matthew 1.1–4.11; Mark 1.1-13; Luke 1.1–4.13
Accounts of the birth, childhood and baptism of Jesus are found in the first chapters of Matthew, Mark and Luke.

58 Jesus' Ministry in Galilee and Journey to Jerusalem

Matthew 4.12–21.1; Mark 1.14–11.1; Luke 4.14–19.27
Jesus spent most of his ministry in Galilee, where he had grown up. He traveled mainly around Lake Galilee, with his home in Capernaum. He may have gone to Jerusalem by way of Perea to avoid going through Samaria.

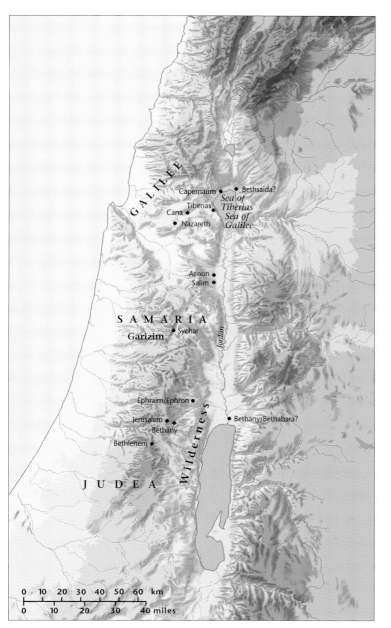

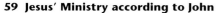

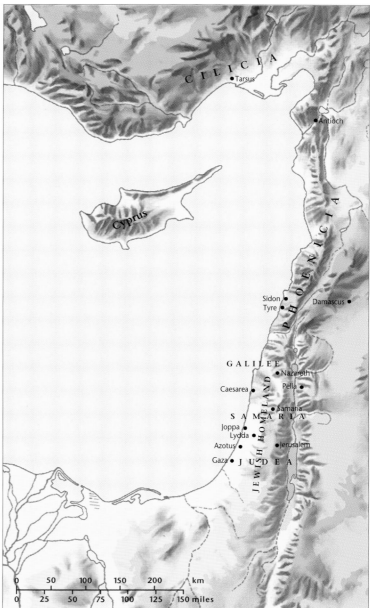

59 Jesus' Ministry according to John

John

The account in the fourth Gospel differs in many ways from that of the first three Gospels. For example, Jesus visited Jerusalem more than once, and different places are named. This evidently represents an independent historical tradition which emphasizes events other than those in the synoptic Gospels.

60 The Early Christian Mission

Acts 2–12

The Christian mission began on Pentecost, when Jews from almost all the areas of the Eastern world and also from Rome received baptism (cf. maps 22 and 23). It was not long before the gospel was being preached beyond Jerusalem in Judea and Samaria, in the towns of the coastal plain and on the seacoast, and even in Damascus and Antioch. Finally, the conversion of Paul marked the beginning of a new phase of the mission.

Shortly before the outbreak of the Jewish War of A.D. 66-70 the members of the early church fled from Jerusalem to Pella across the Jordan.

First Journey

61–64 Paul's Journeys

Acts 9.1-30; 11.25-30; 12.25; 13–14; 15.36–18.22; 18.23–21.17; 27.1–28.16; Galatians 1–2
While traveling to Damascus to persecute Christians there, Paul was himself converted, and in Damascus he was baptized. Then after some time in Arabia he returned to Damascus, visited Jerusalem briefly, and continued actively in evangelism in Cilicia and Syria with Antioch as his base. The church in Antioch sent him together with Barnabas on his first missionary journey. After visiting Jerusalem again he undertook his second and third missionary journeys which took him to Macedonia and Greece with extended periods of activity in Corinth and Ephesus.

During his third and last visit to Jerusalem Paul was arrested and taken first to Caesarea, and then to Rome.

Maps 61–64 illustrate the sequence of events narrated in Acts. Paul's own letters would suggest a different reconstruction of the events.

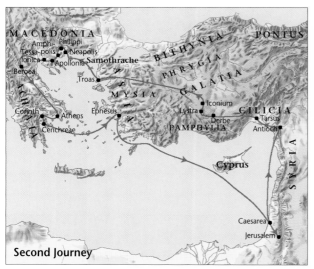

Second Journey

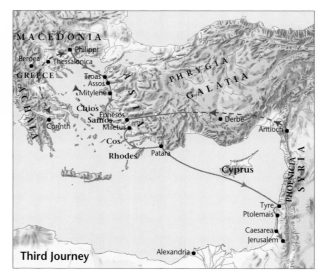

Third Journey

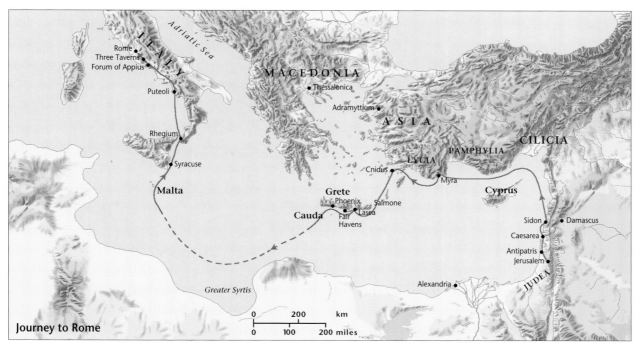

Journey to Rome

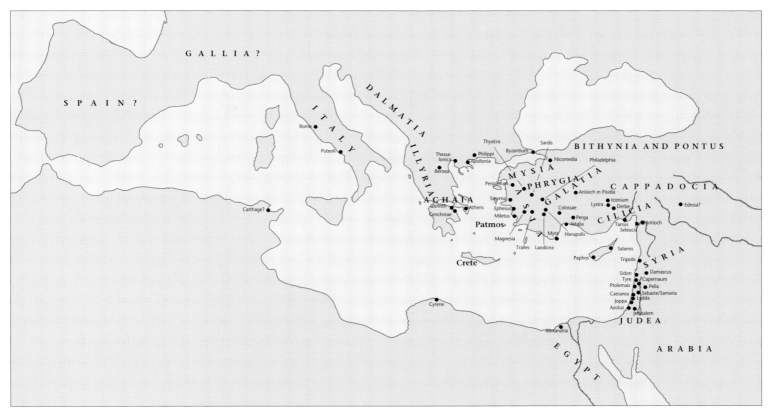

65 The Church ca. A.D. 100

New Testament; 1 Clement
In the time of Emperor Domitian (A.D. 81-96) the church experienced its first period of widespread persecution. By then the church had spread to all levels of society, but it was represented mostly in the eastern parts of the Roman Empire.

66 The Church in the 4th Century A.D.

During the 2nd and 3rd centuries the church expanded through all parts of the Roman Empire, even going beyond its borders in the east. In A.D. 325 Emperor Constantine (A.D.306-337) gave official recognition and support to the church.

The map shows the spread of the church through the empire, naming the principal cities and indicating others by a circle.

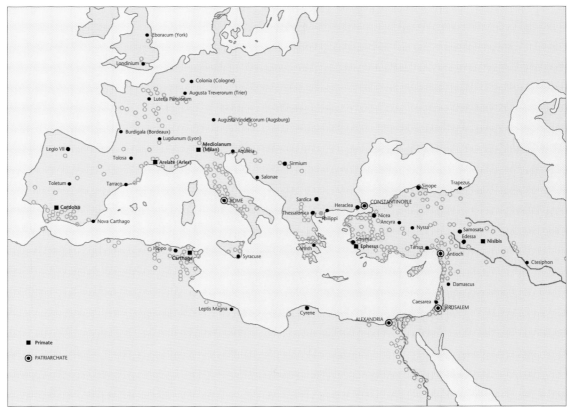

51

Jerusalem

Jerusalem seen from the west. The city is about two thirds of a mile square and enclosed by walls built originally by Hadrian after A.D. 135. The present walls were built by Suleiman the Magnificent (1538-41). Hinnom Valley is in the foreground, and in the shadows beyond the city is Kidron Valley with the Mount of Olives further beyond and the Judean desert in the distance. The oldest part of the city is in the shadows to the right of the Temple Mount.

The city of David was on a ridge south of the Temple Mount and between the Tyropoeon Valley and the Kidron Valley. The upper half of the picture shows the Temple area as expanded by Herod the Great, in the center of which is the Dome of the Rock where the Temple originally stood.

The Kidron Valley viewed from the north. To the right is the southeastern corner of the Temple Mount (the "pinnacle of the temple," cf. Matthew 4.5-7). On the slope to the left Solomon built chapels for his non-Israelite wives.

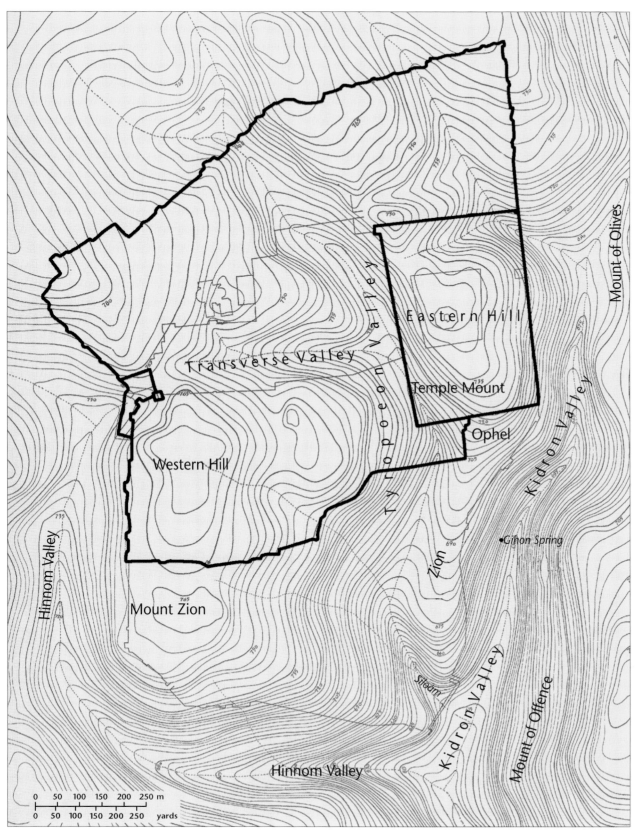

67 Topography

Jerusalem with the biblical place names.

Mount of Olives

Eastern Hill

Transverse Valley

Temple Mount

Tyropoeon Valley

Ophel

Kidron Valley

Western Hill

Zion

Gihon Spring

Hinnom Valley

Mount Zion

Siloam

Kidron Valley

Mount of Offence

Hinnom Valley

| 0 | 50 | 100 | 150 | 200 | 250 m |
| 0 | 50 | 100 | 150 | 200 | 250 yards |

The town was founded in the 3rd millennium B.C., in the early Bronze Age. The original settlement was on the ridge southeast of the present Old City on the Hill of Ophel and just north of the Gihon Spring. Shortly before 1000 B.C. David captured the city and made it his capital. Solomon expanded it northward by building the temple and a palace (see map 73). Under later kings the city expanded westward.

After the exile the settlement was again restricted to the eastern hills, but later expanded to include parts of the western hills, especially under the Maccabees and Hasmoneans.

Herod the Great built a number of public buildings in Jerusalem, most notably the imposing temple known from the New Testament (see map 74).

In the Jewish War of A.D. 66-70 the city and the temple were destroyed, and following the Bar Kochbah rebellion of A.D. 132-135 Jerusalem became a Roman colony under the name Aelia Capitolina. But only two centuries later the Emperor Constantine commissioned a basilica over the tomb of Jesus, which became the center of Christian Jerusalem.

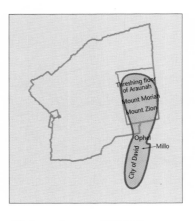

68 Jerusalem in the 3rd and 2nd Millennia B.C.

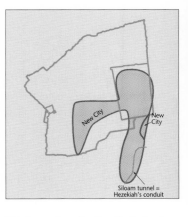

69 Jerusalem ca. 950 B.C.

70 Jerusalem in the Period of the Kings, ca. 950–587 B.C.

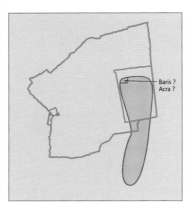

71 Jerusalem in the Time of Nehemiah (Postexilic Jerusalem)

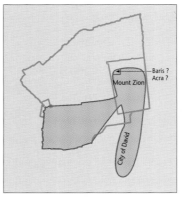

72 Jerusalem in the Hasmonean Period (from the 2nd Century B.C.)

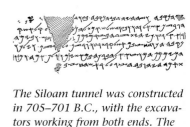

The Siloam tunnel was constructed in 705–701 B.C., with the excavators working from both ends. The inscription records the meeting of the two parties of excavators.

Excavations of extensive terraces on the eastern slopes of David's Jerusalem (Millo?). They were built over houses of the early Iron Age, and were destroyed by Nebuchadnezzar in 587 B.C.

Excavations in Jerusalem have yielded figurines of horses with solar discs dating from the period of King Josiah (cf. 2 Kings 23.11).

The southwestern corner of Herod's temple courtyard. Along the length of the courtyard was a paved street. The large stones fell from the colonnade in the destruction of Jerusalem in A.D. 70.

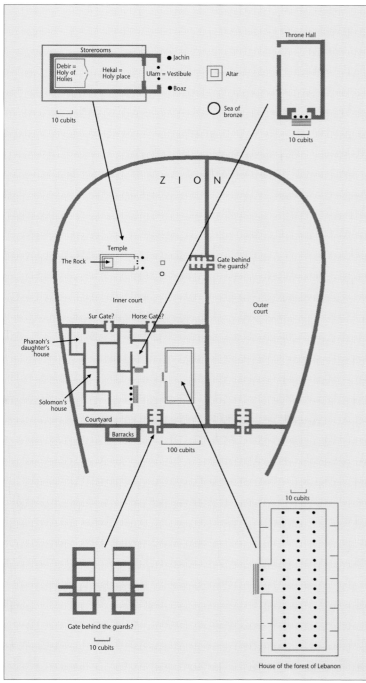

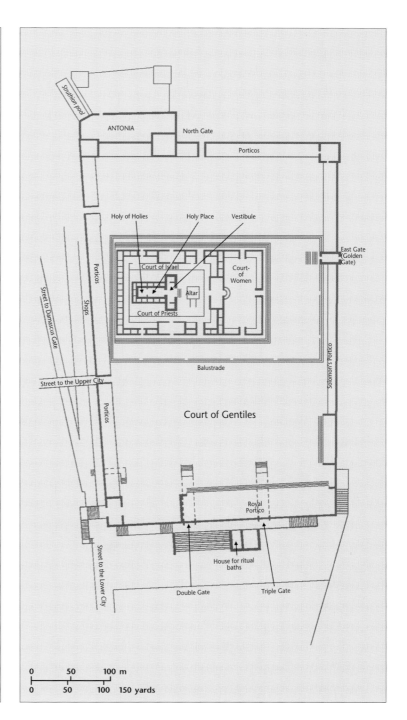

73 Solomon's Temple

1 Kings 6–7; 2 Kings 11; 2 Chronicles 3–4
In 965 B.C. King Solomon began to build the temple north of Jerusalem on the threshing floor of Araunah, also known as Mount Moriah (2 Chronicles 3.1). Although it was seven years in building, it was only a part of a larger palace project which took thirteen years to complete. Little is known about the palace, and this map is a reconstruction based largely on excavations of contemporary palaces and temples in the Middle East.

74 Herod's Temple

Herod the Great began work on the temple in 20/19 B.C., refurbishing Zerubbabel's temple of 520–515 B.C. without interrupting its use, and expanding it on a grand and glorious scale. The building was completed in A.D. 63, and destroyed by Titus in A.D. 70.

The temple was built on a platform raised to a height of 170 feet above the rock base and measuring approximately 920 by 1590 feet.

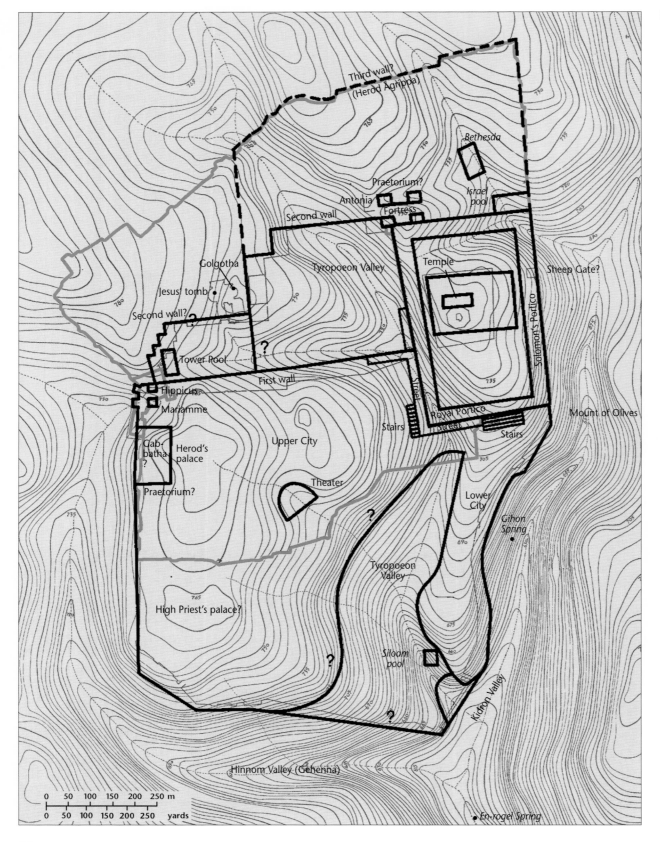

Third wall? (Herod Agrippa)

Bethesda

Praetorium?

Antonia Fortress

Israel pool

Second wall

Tyropoeon Valley

Temple

Sheep Gate?

Golgotha

Jesus' tomb

Second wall?

Solomon's Portico

Tower Pool

First wall

Street

Hippicus

Mariamme

Royal Portico

Stairs

Street

Stairs

Mount of Olives

Gab-batha?

Herod's palace

Upper City

Praetorium?

Theater

Lower City

Gihon Spring

Tyropoeon Valley

High Priest's palace?

Siloam pool

Kidron Valley

Hinnom Valley (Gehenna)

0 50 100 150 200 250 m

0 50 100 150 200 250 yards

En-rogel Spring

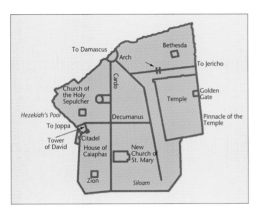

76 Jerusalem in the Byzantine Period

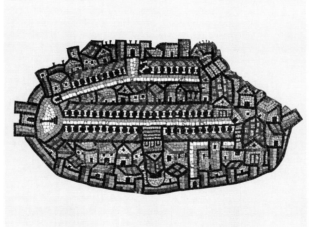

Jerusalem depicted in a mosaic floor at Madaba in Transjordan from the period of Justinian (A.D. 527–565). The view is from the west. At the left the Damascus Gate opens on a plaza with a column; the main street (Cardo) runs through the city. In the foreground is Constantine's Church of the Holy Sepulcher and the Jaffa Gate, while beyond the main street is one street going through the Tyropoeon Valley and one going eastward to St. Stephen's Gate and the Kidron Valley.

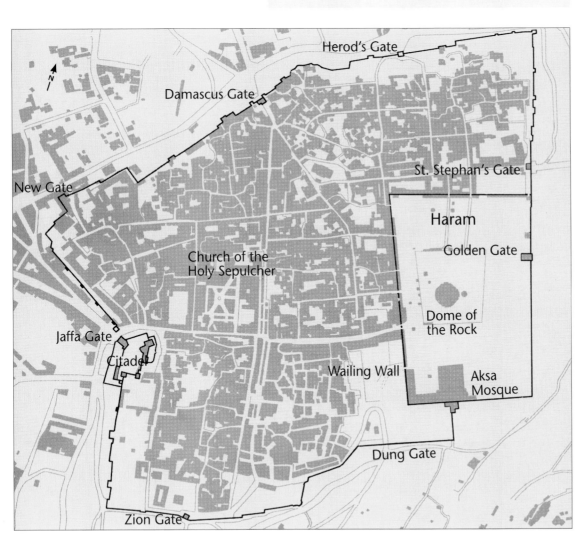

77 The Old City of Jerusalem Today

The Dome of the Rock on the temple mount, built in A.D. 691/692 on the site, where Abraham prepared to sacrifice his son Isaac (or Ishmael, according to Muslim tradition).

The Wailing Wall (Hakotel), a part of the retaining wall of Herod's temple courtyard.

Reference Index Map numbers in italics

Biblical References

Genesis
10 *25*
11.27-25.18 *27*
12.10 *5*
27-35 *28*
32.28 *28*
35.10 *28*
37-50 *29*

Exodus
1 *29*
12.37-19.2 *30*

Numbers
10.11f *30*
12.16 *30*
13-14 *31*
14 *30*
20 *30*
20.17 *2, 6*
21-32 *31*
21.22 *2, 6*
33 *30*

Deuteronomy
1-2 *30*
2-3 *31*

Joshua
2.1-11.15 *32*
12 *31*
13-19 *33*
15.20-62 *44*
18.21-28 *44*
19.40-46 *44*
21 *34*

Judges
1-21 *35*

Ruth
1.1 *5*

1 Samuel
1-7 *35*
9-31 *36*

2 Samuel
2.8f *36*
2-24 *37*
24.5-8 *37*

1 Kings
1-12 *38*
1-2 *37*
4 *38*
6-7 *73*
9 *38*
12-15 *39*
16.23-22 *40*
17-18 *5*

2 Kings
1-13 *40*
13.10-15.7 *41*
15-17 *42*
17.6 *47*
18-20 *43*
18.11 *47*
21-23 *45*
24-25 *46*
24.11-16 *47*
25 *47*

1 Chronicles
4.41-43 *43*
6.39-66 (Vulgate 6.54-81) *34*
9.35-10.14 *36*
11-29 *37*

2 Chronicles
1-9 *38*
3-4 *73*
10-15 *39*
17-24 *40*
25-26 *41*
28.16-21 *42*
29-32 *43*
33-35 *45*
36 *46*

Ezra
2.21-35 *48*
2.59 *47*
8.17 *47*

Nehemiah
3.1-32 *48*
7.26-38 *48*
7.61 *47*
11.25-35 *48*

Isaiah
7-9 *42*
9.1 *2, 6*
10.28-32 *42, 43*
20 *42, 43*
36-39 *43*

Jeremiah
27.3 *46*
29 *47*
32 *46*
37-39 *46*
42-46 *47*
52 *46, 47*

Ezekiel
1.1-3 *47*
3.15 *47*

Amos *41*

Micah
1.8-16 *43*

1 Maccabees
1-16 *50*
15.16, 22 f *23*

2 Maccabees *50*

Matthew
1-4.11 *57*
4.12-21.1 *58*

Mark
1.1-13 *57*
1.14-11.1 *58*

Luke
1-4.13 *57*
4.14-19.29 *58*

John *59*

Acts
2-12 *60*
2.9-11 *23*
9.1-30 *61-64*
11.25-30 *61-64*
12.25 *61-64*
13-14 *61-64*
15.36-18.22 *61-64*
18.23-21.17 *61-64*
27.1-28.16 *61-64*

Galatians
1-2 *61-64*

Non-Biblical References

Amarna Archives *14*

Karnak Temple Inscription *39*

Jubilees 8-9 *26*

1 Clement *65*

Geographical Index Map numbers in italics